D0341108

JESUS
and the Politics
of Violence

George R. Edwards

HARPER & ROW, PUBLISHERS
New York, Evanston, San Francisco, London

To Jean,
Riley, Virginia, and John

FIRST EDITION

LIBRARY OF CONGRESS CATALOG CARD NUMBER: 70-183635

CONTENTS

iii

PREFACE

Biblical interpretation concerns not only the ancient but also the modern scene. So this book endeavors to link the twentieth century and the first. Violence as a problem of our time receives primary attention in Chapters 1 and 5, though the biblical questions of Chapters 2 through 4 are raised in a manner that indicates their contemporary significance. The reader will thread his way through the discussion with greater ease by looking up the biblical references when the translation is not cited.

This book was written during a sabbatical year (1970–71) from my professorship in New Testament Studies at Louisville Presbyterian Theological Seminary in Louisville, Kentucky. My thanks to the Seminary for this leave and for many other things are deeply felt. A supplemental grant was graciously provided by the Advanced Religious Studies Foundation, enabling my family and me to reside for the year in Toronto, Canada. We found it a very pleasant place to be.

The Rev. R. Grant Bracewell, librarian at Emmanuel College of Victoria University in the University of Toronto, and his assistants, Mrs. Moira Allen and Georges Bonneau, extended numerous courtesies and prompt aid in the acquisition and use of books and articles.

Biblical quotations are, except where otherwise designated, from the Revised Standard Version. Except for a few articles from *Interpretation* where the translator is not given, the translators of foreign texts are named. In all other cases the translations are mine.

August 1971   GEORGE R. EDWARDS

I. VIOLENCE: DEFINITIONS
IN TRANSITION

Violence. If we must, let's talk about it, but by seeing it first for what
it is: a word. A word used by those who elaborated and imposed the
language: the masters. According to how the word will serve them, it
can signify God's will; used against them, it can become a sign of shame
and degradation. When white men use violence, violence is good. When
blacks use it, they are considered animals. However, it so happens that
the blacks have exposed the tricks of the language, as they have exposed
religious tricks, legal shams and social deformities. Blacks aren't afraid
of words any more, regardless of the coloration that whites might give
them.

It is evident that recommending non-violence to blacks is an effort to
retain the Christian vocabulary which has kept them imprisoned in
passivity for so long. However Christian the whites are, they don't feel
guilty about using guns: that is violence. Asking blacks in America to
be non-violent means that whites are demanding a Christian virtue which
they themselves do not possess. That means that whites are once again
trying to dupe the blacks.[1]

These angry words of Jean Genet vividly etch the painful
dilemma in which the conscience of man is caught. This dilemma
exists wherever serious attention is given to the issues of justice
and peace.

No reflective person can deny that violence is a word subjected to frequent manipulations, depending on the passions and

1

commitments of those using the term. The deaths inflicted by the
National Guard at Kent State University in the spring of 1970,
though judged unnecessary by the FBI, provoked no general outcry about criminal violence.[2] Shortly afterward, on May 14, 1970,
the shooting of students at Jackson State College in Jackson,
Mississippi, passed in the white community as an act of legitimate
police control, although the Scranton Commission referred to the
fusillade of twenty-eight seconds that killed two and wounded
twelve as "completely unwarranted and unjustified."[3]

When one observes the myriad devices by which an indiffer-
ent majority frustrates progress toward equal opportunity, aided
by its elected officials, he understands black militancy not only in
America but throughout the nonwhite world. He seriously questions whether the scruple about violence is not after all a mere
piece of political reaction, a convenient tool for keeping deprived
people submissive to their masters. Certainly, if the advocacy of
nonviolence is only a device of white supremacy, its exposure can
do no harm. On the other hand, few would grant that the issue of
violence is resolved so easily as the statement of Genet would indicate.

A Conventional Definition

Even if violence is only a word, it may be accorded the right
of definition. We begin with a definition based on usage: Violence
is physical force resulting in injury or destruction of property or
persons in violation of general moral belief or civil law. Here the
etymological connection of the term with the Latin *vis* (through
violentia), meaning physical strength or force, is maintained. It
also retains its usual morally negative connotation.

Biblical usage has certainly enforced the moral disfavor associated with violence. Mandelkern's Hebrew concordance lists sixty-eight (sixty for the noun; eight for the verb) instances of the Hebrew root ḤMS in the Old Testament. Translators generally render this root with some form of the word "violence." In at least sixty-seven of the occurrences the aspect of moral disfavor is obvious.[4] ḤMS is typically used in the parallelism of Genesis 6:11: "Now the earth was corrupt in God's sight, and the earth was filled with violence." These words set the stage for the Priestly account of the deluge in Genesis 6:9–22, but the same connotation prevails throughout the prophetic and hagiographal books as well. Psalm 140:1–3 may be taken as normative: "Deliver me, O Lord, from evil men; preserve me from violent men, who plan evil things in their heart, and stir up wars continually. They make their tongue sharp as a serpent's, and under their lips is the poison of vipers."

The Greek root *bia* (violence) is not frequently found in the New Testament. The problematical text Matthew 11:12 (= Luke 16:16), "From the days of John the Baptist until now the kingdom of heaven has suffered violence, and men of violence take it by force," does employ cognate forms of *bia*. Some interpreters have construed "men of violence" as referring to the Zealots, guerrilla fighters for Jewish independence from Rome.[5] While that is not impossible, it is by no means certain. It is certain that Matthew attaches a morally negative sense to "has suffered violence" and "men of violence" and that Luke has adapted the text underlying Matthew, introducing an inoffensive and mitigating idea.[6] Whatever the correct interpretation of Matthew 11:12 may be, it is sufficient to observe that this noted text does not break the pattern established by the Old Testament idea of violence.[7]

The Eisenhower Commission defined violence as "behavior designed to inflict physical injury to people or damage to property," which adds the element of forethought or intention to the injurious action.[8] The report of the commission goes on to distinguish between violence and force, defining the latter as "the actual

or threatened use of violence to compel others to do what they
might not otherwise do." The report seems less explicit on the
moral nuance of the terms: "Force, like violence, can be judged
good or bad," an observation that shows the strain under which
the conventional definition now labors. This points up the necessity of clarifying what has been happening in the contemporary
language of violence.

Traditional Definitions under Stress

Language is historically conditioned. In our time the awareness has increased that violence is not necessarily physical in the
overt, visible sense.

In *Black Power*, Carmichael and Hamilton distinguish between individual and institutional racism.[9] Individual racism
refers to overt acts such as the bombing of a Negro church, a
lynching, or stoning or shooting into a house occupied by blacks.
Institutional racism puts the deed, so to speak, out of sight: I did
not and would not bomb a church, lynch anyone, or shoot into a
house. Yet whites are still patrons of institutional racism in that
they live in all-white neighborhoods (so maintained by covert or
written agreements), go to all-white schools and churches, belong
to all-white unions, and follow employment practices that are dis-
criminatory.

These distinctions also apply to violence. Removed from
visible participation in violence, we do not feel responsible for it.
Its palatability is thus increased. This institutional aspect of violence renders inadequate the traditional definitions.

Franz Fanon, in *The Wretched of the Earth*, has pilloried the
institutional violence of colonialism and stoutly defended the
necessity of violence in the process of liberation.[10] While personal
violence against the body or property of someone in a less indus-
trialized country of Africa or Asia had earned general moral dis-

approval by the second half of our century, economic and even territorial colonization continued to enjoy widespread endorsement. Fanon emphasizes that settlers and colonists have not conveyed to the natives their rights of autonomy out of sheer benevolence. Only guns and terrorism rightly employed have won these rights. This is how America felt about Britain's rule in 1776, so Fanon should be no surprise to Americans.

Colin Morris in Zambia has also given cogent expression to the nature of institutional violence expressed in colonialism: "To starve people is violence; to rob them of their dignity and self-respect is violence; to deny to them their political rights or discriminate against them is violence. Elaborate structures of violence make a terrorist what he is, and he faces them as the weaker adversary."[11]

The point of this is that moral belief and civil law are not yet prepared to mount serious opposition to institutional forms of violence. The present struggle going on in human society over the meaning and morality of violence arises from the multitudinous ways in which morality and law are invoked to legitimate injustice against and exploitation of the less powerful. Charles West illustrates the ambiguity of language when he defines violence as it is used within the "covenant" of American public life:

Violence is harm done to another outside the rules of conflict which such a society sets up. It may even be the redress of grievances by means which society does not permit. For example, the occupation of a building by sit-in protestors may be regarded as violence, but not the planned eviction of the tenants from their homes at the expiration of their leases so that the landlord can tear down the building for his profit. Again, if the government of a poor country confiscates without compensation a foreign-owned business, its action may be called violent, while the owner's systematic retention of the disproportionate profit from his enterprise, which led to the action, will not be so labelled.[12]

"The rules of conflict which such a society sets up" have to do with both morality and law. West makes it clear that the covenant on which the liberal society rests assumes that the means of redress are provided within the constitutional system. From both Marx and Freud, however, has come the increasingly universalized awareness that a great gulf is often fixed between what we say to ourselves or one another in our explicit language and what the nonverbal facts of the case are. From the viewpoint of our generation it seems both morally and legally impossible, but it is nevertheless a fact, that the men who framed the Declaration of Independence were also slaveholders. When, therefore, contemporary blacks write a manifesto or a new declaration of independence or engage in acts that threaten the covenant of public life, it must be understood that many of them categorically do not feel that they have been sharers in the American covenant or participants in the public contract.

In affairs among nations, the gap between professions and practice is even more extensive than is the case in domestic issues. Constitutional governments provide at least a language by which moral and legal debate about violence can be carried on. When, however, major world powers flaunt or circumvent even the inchoative forms of international covenants, by what logic is international violence to be discussed? Thus, in recent years of American history, the peculiar power of the presidency and the National Security Council—one thinks of the Bay of Pigs decision, the action in Dominica, and especially the war in Vietnam as examples—functions even in a liberal democratic society in ways that not only contravene explicit provisions of international agreements (such as the second article of the United Nations Charter and the fifteenth article of the Charter of the Organization of American States), but also effectively nullify democratic participation in such decisions. The Pentagon Papers fully illustrate this. When, moreover, legislative instruments such as the Tonkin Bay Resolution and the Selective Service laws compel citizens to implement the violence that such decisions require, it should be no surprise that violent reactions in the society are generated.

It does not follow, of course, that peace and order would prevail if only societies would observe more strictly the moral and legal rules of conflict that they establish. This is because institutional violence is given legitimacy within the society's rules of conflict. We have, for example, numerous communities where white supremacy effects laws on segregation, even in places where blacks may constitute a majority. Custom or law in male-dominated societies decrees the subservience of women. The injustice that spawns violence is not confined, furthermore, to the machinations of ruling minorities. As Alexis de Tocqueville philosophized, it may be enthusiastically endorsed by popular vote.

The rules of conflict in warfare are notoriously capricious in this regard. The death of elderly people, women, and children may be regarded as tolerable in the morality of war when these deaths are inflicted from the air, inflicted as it were from a proper distance. But the My Lai deaths, inflicted on the ground at close range, constitute atrocities. It is also reasonably questioned why those who committed these atrocities are any guiltier of bloody violence than those of us at home who made them agents of the atrocious policies that we and our representatives conceived.

The complexities we have canvassed already evoke the cynical conclusion that the word violence is indeed nothing more than a cudgel to be employed by adversaries in the struggle for power. The terminology of violence has been punched and pushed into innumerable shapes and uses. Each of the following propositions may be, in context, quite expressive; education is violence; technology is violence; matrimony is violence; boredom is violence; taxation is violence; work is violence. The list can be multiplied, and the predicate nominative ("violence") can sit in the subject position. But it is also clear that words that acquire too many meanings eventually have no meaning at all.

The proposal to discuss Jesus and the politics of violence bears the hope of clarifying from the religious angle the language of violence. Within religious communions themselves there is dis-

agreement on the meaning and morality of violence. It will perhaps prove some advantage to public life if churchmen can reassess the biblical materials that bear upon this problem.

Christians for Violence

Jacques Ellul has devoted considerable attention to "Today's
Christians for Violence."[13] Among these he lists Richard Shaull,
Arthur Rich, the Frères du Monde (a group of French Franciscans
directed by a Father Maillard), Canon Gonzales Ruiz, Camilo
Torres (the noted Colombian priest killed in an armed uprising in
1966), Thomas Melville (member of the Maryknoll Society who
was expelled from Guatemala), and others less famed.

Ellul is not unaware that the viewpoint and activity of such
persons are frequently misrepresented, even though the summary
style of his discussion fails to explain the experience and reasoning that underlie their positions. One may justly cavil at the
phrase "Christians for Violence" in and of itself, since very few
men, Christian or not, consider themselves advocates of violence.

It would be fairer to say that these and other Christians
whose views we discuss are not advocates of violence but reluctantly accept its necessity when all nonviolent means have been
exhausted. At the same time, in a world where nobody advocates
violence, it is necessary to ask why the frequency and magnitude
of violence keep rising. It is also something of an innovation in
our time that the writings of religious men seek to show the necessity of violence where other means fail.

Willis Elliott published an article in 1968 called "No Alternative to Violence."[14] His argument is that the correction of injustice against the Negro in the United States will not come about
without a discriminating use of violence against property (only).

He carefully disapproves violence to persons, for what appear to be tactical reasons, but asserts that "blacks threatening to destroy, and actually destroying, white property is essential to the black cause."

Elliott's use of biblical materials is interesting. The Exodus, central to Old Testament salvation history, is bathed in violence. God himself perpetrates it in defense of his people. This shows the intimate relation between violence and redemption. In the New Testament, Jesus is also the agent of redemption by violence: in his proclamation of the imminent, violent inbreaking of the Kingdom of God against the powers of evil and on behalf of the poor (Luke 6:20); in his vision of the destroyed Temple (Matt. 24:2); in the cursing of the fig tree and the cleansing of the Temple as "signs of the coming divine violence in nature . . . and society." Furthermore, "In Christianity, what parallels the Exodus Event is Jesus' Resurrection—parallels it not in cultic significance but as a divine violent intervention (an *uprising* (*anastasis*))." Jesus' expectation that God would come through soon with the necessary violence opens to Christians the option of violence while remaining faithful to Christ. This is particularly the case in that Jesus' expectation of supernatural intervention did not materialize. The ambiguity of Jesus' attitude on violence is represented in the two texts, "Put up your sword" (Matt. 26:52) and "I came to bring a sword" (Matt. 10:34).

With these premises it is not at all clear why Elliott goes on to say that violence is almost never appropriate, or why violence against persons should be disapproved. It wasn't just horses that were wiped out in the Red Sea saga.

Elliott abstains from polemics against nonviolence, but there is a growing volume of such polemics in the liberation literature. LeRoi Jones provides an example:

The unity I desire would be most apparent when most Black People realized that the murderous philosophies of the Western white man take many curious forms. And that one of the most bizarre methods the man has yet to utilize [sic] against the black people is to instruct large masses of black people that they are to control their tempers, turn the other cheek, etc. in the presence of, but even more so under the feet and will of, the most brutal killers the world has yet produced.[15]

Jones goes on to affirm that "even the black man who preaches nonviolence is essentially functioning under the trance of white people." He also invokes the example of the Exodus to repudiate the nonviolent phase of the American civil rights struggle.

If the program of black liberation includes, as Elliott affirms, steps "to strike Congress and American business with the fears of chaos" and to "make the white elephant think he's sinking in black quicksand," it is already evident that smashing a few selected storefronts is not going to turn the tide.

There is no question, of course, that the Exodus story included not only the slaughter of the Egyptians but also the conquest and dispossession of the Canaanites, making way for the establishment of the Hebrew commonwealth. If one wishes to carry out some kind of ethical analogue on the basis of the Exodus, it is not clear why the Canaanites should not correspond to the contemporary, nonwhite, dispossessed peoples. Certainly the conquest of the American Indian by European whites in colonial America was executed under auspices of a kind of divinely sanctioned Manifest Destiny. As Richard M. Brown wrote for the Eisenhower Commission, this conquest effectively fashioned America's subsequent inclinations toward solutions written in human blood:

Broken treaties, unkept promises, and the slaughter of defenseless women and children all, along with the un-European atrocity of taking scalps, continued to characterize the white American's mode of dealing with the Indians. The effect on our national character has not been a healthy one; it has done much to shape our proclivity to violence.[16]

It is instructive to impose the Exodus paradigm on the current problems of the Near East. The remarkable growth of the

Zionist idea did not occur in a vacuum. Guilt over the tragic results of anti-Semitism, especially during National Socialism in
Germany, stimulated the "Christian west" in its latent biblical assumption that Palestine belongs to the Jews.

But, obviously, Palestinian residents displaced by the establishment and expansion of Israel feel that they are in the position of the exploited. They conclude as a result that terrorism
applied against Israel under such conditions cannot fail to receive divine sanction. What has prevailed in the Near East under
the auspices of a very old form of political logic is escalation
toward disaster. If, moreover, the Arabs and Palestinians with
Soviet aid should eventually conquer Israel, or Israel with American aid should nullify·further UAR or Palestinian harrassment,
what would such a result have to do with divine providence or
moral justice?

The same applies to the clash of races in America. Let us assume that advocates of "liberating violence" should gain the
ascendancy in the black community by a combination of public
apathy, inept political leadership, and unrelieved frustrations in
the hopes of the blacks. Let us further assume that mounting civil
disorder should finally yield to a state of guerilla warfare, some
whites aiding the blacks, some blacks joining the champions of
law and order. Even with aid from outside sources, which black
liberators might be able to muster, it does not seem likely that
such a revolution could defeat the forces of repression, although,
as we are often reminded, "substantial parts of America could be
torn down." What moral or theological wisdom could be pronounced on this disaster? Would it confirm that God is on the side
of the white supremacists?

Now that pronouncements about "the failure of nonviolence"
(to achieve black liberation) have become popular, the stage is
being set quite elaborately for new dramas demonstrating once
again the failure of violence. The rhetoric of revolution and the
politics of repression are as old as history itself, so much so, in
fact, that one senses in the contemporary pattern of confronta-

tions an element as inexorable as it is repetitious. The violence of the Hebrew Exodus, in sum, especially with its subsequent conquest of Canaan, is not a model that spreads much light in the contemporary darkness.

As to Elliott's use of the New Testament, here is the blunt fact: There is not a single text in all the New Testament in which *anastasis* (resurrection) means "uprising" in the sense suggested by Elliott. Luke 2:34 is no exception. Liddell and Scott in fact do not list even for nonbiblical Greek the meaning "insurrection" for *anastasis*.[17] The Greek words for insurrection are *apostasis, bia, epanastasis, stasis*. Yet, by the logic of "No Alternative to Violence," Jesus' resurrection validates armed insurrection. This reasoning echoes a passage in *The Passover Plot*, where Schonfield affirms that "One of the planks in Paul's platform had been *anastasis Christou* (the resurrection of Christ), which could equally be understood as 'Messianic uprising.' "[18] The phrase could be understood in this sense in Pauline literature only by someone wholly unfamiliar with what Paul is talking about.

Elliott's juxtaposing of "put up your sword" (Matt. 26:52) and "I came to bring a sword" (Matt. 10:34) cannot, furthermore, yield the doublemindedness of which he speaks when attention is paid to the context. Matthew 10:35 ("For I have come to set a man against his father, and a daughter-in-law against her mother-in-law") indicates that the "sword" of verse 34 is a metaphorical reference to family divisions. Luke 12:51 is the parallel to Matthew 10:34. It reads: "Do you think that I have come to give peace on earth? No, I tell you, but rather division." It is likely again in this instance that Luke has mitigated the implication of the underlying text. The sixteenth saying of the Gospel of Thomas states: "I have come to cast divisions upon the earth, fire, sword, war," which may constitute a text prior to both Matthew and Luke and from which they conveyed what suited them.[19] Despite the added militancy of this logion 16 (*viz.*, "war"), the metaphorical element is sustained even there by the clause that follows: ". . . for there shall be five in a house; there

will be three against two and two against three; the father against
the son and the son against the father, and they will stand alone
(or, as monks)."²⁰ From the time of Micah 7 such family divisions were a common theme of apocalyptic thought.

The fulcrum of Elliott's argument is that since Jesus mistakenly anticipated the imminent inbreaking of the Kingdom of
God with power—Elliott understands this to mean "with violence"
—movements for social change are therefore entitled to effect the
kingdom's approach by the selective property violence called for
by the situation. But even if we grant the implicit assumption in
this that the Kingdom of God is to be equated with the socio-
political model projected by Elliott, it is too much to propose that
the tactic for social change should operate contrary to the tactic
of Jesus because he misunderstood eschatology. In short, except
for the unexplained reservation about violence to persons, Elliott's
social program for Christianity seems to provide nothing from its
New Testament roots that is not more readily accessible in the
usual dogmas of political revolution.

Christianity and Third World Violence

The Reverend Colin Morris is president of the United
Church of Zambia. In his book, *Unyoung, Uncoloured, Unpoor*
(1969), he reflects on the failure of nonviolence and the necessity
of violent revolution. The wounds of white colonialism are so
deep in the African consciousness that any questions about the
means of liberation would appear to be moralistic. Yet Morris
begins his book with a letter in which an African churchman
himself raises the conflict of conscience imposed by the fight for
freedom (in Rhodesia) on the one hand and the scruple about
violence raised by a Christian tradition on the other hand. Morris
wants to reassure this inquirer that violence in the fight for freedom is certainly not in conflict with Christian belief.

Morris extols the violence supported by Bonhoeffer in the 1944 plot to bomb Hitler:

I, for one, believe that his explanation of the theology behind the bomb plot might have more to say to our time. The new theology for which the church is searching may be hidden in that violent deed of Bonhoeffer's which misfired and not in his musings about God without religion. Any Christian, tasting the sulphur which hangs in the air of our time, could wish for a theology of violence from the pen of a great theologian who dared to strike and paid for his temerity with his life.[21]

Bonhoeffer's complicity in the Stauffenberg conspiracy reminds one how premeditated styles of behavior may melt away in the heat of existential involvement. The contemplation beforehand of moral responsibility is as necessary, however, for intelligent morality as the absence of it guarantees moral rashness. Morris himself expresses some reservations about tyrannicide.

One of these has to do (in the Stauffenberg conspiracy) with the element of timing. What if the bomb had been planted ten years earlier, before the "gas chambers had blackened the sky and Europe's cities were aflame?" Morris answers: "If the Christian can only be sure that he is right to use violence when evil screams its true nature to the world, he will invariably strike too late." That is, Hitler should have been stopped earlier by a more wordly perception of what things were coming to. But in 1934, Morris concedes, Hitler was by no means regarded as the monstrous evil he was in 1944. If the bombing had come earlier, Bonhoeffer would have been assigned a place in history alongside Lee Harvey Oswald.

Morris also faults the inexpert character of the attempt on Hitler's life: "good theologians make bad assassins, or . . . the Lutheran pietism of the 1930s was a poor springboard for bold action." Thus, while the blow aimed at Hitler missed its mark, "others in that map room were destroyed, some of them honorable soldiers."[22] It is certain that many well-intentioned acts, including those designed for nonviolent execution, may result in violence or even death due to unforeseeable accidents within the target area. We may rightly question, however, whether weapons of violence do not overtly possess such capabilities that these derivative effects can be excused merely because they are unintended. The courage of Bonhoeffer is not compromised by these observations. They intend to put more sharply the very issue that Morris himself raises.

What Morris has to say about the violence of Jesus is particularly relevant to our major theme. He relates that S. G. F. Brandon's *Jesus and the Zealots* did not come to his attention until he had already, on grounds of political instinct, rejected "the orthodox view of the pacifist Christ." Brandon, with "massive and wideranging scholarship," adds biblical acumen to Morris's political instinct to corroborate endorsement of the violent Jesus, whose "prophetic mantle . . . passes to Marx, Lenin, and Mao, and then to Castro, Ho Chi Minh, and Torres," though "none is entitled to wear it for long."[23] Morris parallels Brandon so extensively in his comments on Jesus that the following tabulation results:

1. Jesus echoed from his heart the Zealot's invincible love of liberty.
   Morris, p. 105.   Brandon, p. 65.

2. Taking up the cross (Mark 8:34), signifying a political fate, was adopted in Christianity from Zealotism and signified defiance of Rome.
   Morris, p. 106.   Brandon, pp. 57, 145, 269, 344, 356.

3. Jesus attacked Pharisees, Herodians, and Sadducees, *but not the Zealots*.
   Morris, p. 107.   Brandon, pp. 200, 327.

4. Jesus' call of the Zealot Simon as disciple shows he was pro-Zealot.
   Morris, p. 107.   Brandon, pp. 42–43, 201, 243.

5. The Barabbas amnesty (Mark 15:6–15), historically unsupportable, only shows Mark's pro-Roman, anti-Jewish bias.
   Morris, pp. 108–11.   Brandon, pp. 258–64.

6. The tribute question (Mark 12:13–17) shows Jesus at one with the Zealots in advocating insurrection against Rome.
    Morris, pp. 112–13.   Brandon, pp. 224, 270–71, 345–49.

7. The triumphal entry (Mark 11:1–7) was a demonstration carefully planned by Jesus to signify his potential messiahship.
    Morris, pp. 114–16.   Brandon, pp. 349–50, 353.

8. The temple cleansing (Mark 11:15–19) was an act of political violence aimed at the overthrow of the priestly aristocracy.
    Morris, pp. 116–17.   Brandon, pp. 332–39.

9. Despite Matthew 26:52, realistic interpretation of the armed clash in Gethsemane shows Jesus' kinship to Zealotism.
    Morris, pp. 118–19.   Brandon, pp. 203, 340–42.

Although Morris and Brandon diverge in certain details under items 6 and 9 in the foregoing, it is clear that in biblical matters, Morris stands or falls with Brandon. Later in this book Brandon's work will be placed under fuller scrutiny. We pause to relate in connection with item 3 above, however, that this same argument from silence was used to make Jesus into an Essene (the only Jewish sect not named in the Gospels), and Schweitzer in the *Quest* correctly subsumes these "lives of Jesus" based on the Essene theory under the category of fiction. Morris (who disclaims any biblical expertise) depends so uncritically on Brandon for his moral and political premises that he demonstartes aptly the necessity for careful inquiry into what Brandon has written. Before turning to that, however, we wish to show the relationship between "violence" and "power."

Violence and Power

In 1969 Adolf Berle published the second edition of his book *Power*. He possesses both the experiential and academic acquaintance with the political aspects of power to give his work an exemplary character.

In a prologue and epilogue, Berle draws upon the mythology of Hesiod's *Theogony* to establish a transcendental framework for the philosophy of power. In the beginning, Zeus subdued the chaotic forces: He bound and castrated Chronus; he fought the Cyclops; he subdued the half-nymph goddesses, and he banned the whole unruly pack to Tartarus. But the forces of chaos are not passive. They try to upset the balance of order in the heavenly hierarchy, particularly through the agency of Pallas Athena, whose wisdom, reason, and knowledge are as necessary to the rule of Zeus as her self-assertion is a threat to him.

Incorporating priests and religion (along with scientists, educators, and technologists) under the rubric of Athena, Berle comments that the day when prophets toppled thrones is departed now and that even the highest technologists stand under the political potentates, a point evidenced in the fact that Truman, advised by "a committee of eminent but not too intelligent Americans" overrode the scruples of scientists about the use of the A-bomb on human targets.[24]

Berle's analysis is attended by a pronounced nostalgia in the final section of his book, "The Decline of Power" (written during the 1968 student unrest at Columbia University where he was then teaching). He locates "the fundamental problem in America today" in what may be called our ideological decline or the erosion of that idea structure that gives power its coherence. His catalogue of the operations of power in the American presidency, the industrial corporation, the Supreme Court, the Pentagon, and other components of the American system is moved by the desire to correct the disorder (exemplified in the student revolt) into which we have fallen.

Throughout, Berle asumes the Machiavellian notion of power and he regards *The Prince* as "the greatest single study of power on record." He summarizes the essence of Machiavellian nationalism vis-à-vis the question of international order as follows:

Its content is simple. Each state must protect and forward its territory, its economic welfare advantages, and its military strength; this is the highest morality for princes and power holders. Not, it will be noticed, that each state must merely defend itself; rather, each must aggrandize or at least strengthen itself where it can. In pursuit of these goals, success justifies measures; the attained end justifies the means.[25]

Though Berle records the fact that *"The Prince* was condemned by Catholics and Protestants alike because it made no adequate bow toward any moral system," it does not deter his enthusiasm for the Machiavellian politic.[26]

These brief descriptions are sufficient to bring us to the center of the power issue. Plainly put, the bold application of violence is a self-evident necessity if the structure of power is to be maintained against revolutionary deviations. The name of this in international politics is containment.

Berle remains wholly silent on the Bay of Pigs operation, although it is well known that he was a part of the meeting of the National Security Council on April 4, 1961, at which the decision to go into the Bay of Pigs was finally made.[27] Since the only objections to this exercise in containment seem to have been those raised by Senator Fulbright and Arthur Schlesinger, Jr., it is hard to take Berle seriously when he states in connection with the Caribbean: "Americans can readily accept a regime not based on private enterprise and private property. . . ."[28] Since he was also on the National Security Council or high in advisory councils when the Kennedy policies on Vietnam were laid and executed (again, without stated objections in *Power*), it follows that what has been done in Vietnam, just as in Korea, Dominica, Greece, the Congo, and in various countries of Latin America, constitutes a coherent manifestation of the philosophy of power. It also follows that in the absence of a "stronger" United Nations (for which Berle voices certain hopes), the continued practice of Machiavellian power remains inevitable. One is driven, therefore, to the conclusion that what Berle bemoans as "the fundamental problem in America today" is decline of ideological support for the particular scheme of order versus chaos that American policy has reflected in recent years.

The problem must be carried a step further. As Erich Fromm has demonstrated in *May Man Prevail?*, the terms of the power-over-chaos paradigm remain exactly the same when one thinks from the Marxist side of the power struggle. Now the capitalist societies represent chaos and the Marxist ones order. Zeus changes sides. So the bloody repression in Hungary in 1956 and the (providentially) less bloody repression in Czechoslovakia in 1968 become the normative consequence of the realism of power from the other side of the wall, right down to the documentation of counterrevolutionary conspiracies. Given the ideological presuppositions of the cold war, it does not take a prophet to answer the question whether man shall prevail. Caught between two juggernauts of self-righteous power, each claiming ultimate moral authority for its own brand of peace and order, the prospect for man's future is reduced to zero.

From this standpoint, the decline of ideological support for national power lamented by Berle is not, as he states, a signal of disaster, but of new religious possibilities. Perhaps Berle remembers the day in 1941 when theologians and churchmen closed ranks behind Reinhold Niebuhr to provide a supportive idea system through whose patronage America's power could ascend the ladder to fulfillment. Athena did then stay in her place.

But that happy coalition has suffered almost continuous erosion since the war in Korea. Though the post-Niebuhrian ethicists (one thinks of Paul Ramsey or David Little) made strong efforts through 1967 or 1968 to provide moral validation for the Vietnam war, Reinhold Niebuhr, as an example of the new mood in theology, had categorically repudiated the war, and religious support for it could never be consolidated despite the vigorous efforts of the Johnson and Nixon administrations.[29] As the violence of power continues to manifest itself, the academic and religious community continues to withdraw support for Machiavellian political ideals.

The struggle in America and in the world to lay bare the causes of violence has sharpened the awareness that the ideas of religion and nation fostered by Reinhold Niebuhr in 1940 are ill suited to the requirements for survival that we now face. Indeed, with respect to the foundations of Christianity, it will be argued subsequently that the violence connected with ethnic and national power has so distanced Christian practice from the ethical models propounded in the Gospels that Christians have lost their claims to credibility. In so far as the student revolt summons us to discover the meaning and cure of violence, it is a sign not of death, but life.

II. JESUS AND THE ZEALOTS:
A MATTHAEAN APPROACH

The recovery of the historical Jesus from the Gospel records is a task so difficult that few scholars today are brash enough to undertake it. Bultmann states the problem in the following emphatic terms: "We can know almost nothing about the life and personality of Jesus, since the earliest Christian sources show no interest in either, are moreover, fragmentary and often legendary; and other sources about Jesus do not exist."[1] In *The Quest of the Historical Jesus*, Albert Schweitzer expresses a corresponding view in his metaphor of the railroad ticket: There are no "through" tickets from the first station to the last that provide an objective explanation of Jesus, tying his life understandably together from baptism to crucifixion.[2] Each episode of the tradition stands alone, on its own feet, so the reader must get off at each stop and get another ticket.

It is, however, a matter of dispute how well such writers observe their own precautions. Schweitzer, for example, authors what may finally be judged as a life of Jesus, filling in the lacunae of the history with the eschatological explanation.[3] Bultmann also distinguishes at numerous points between authentic sayings of Jesus and those ascribed to him by the church or the evangelists. His familiar stratification of 1) early Palestinian tradition, 2) churchly theology, and 3) editorial commentary significantly eclipses the figure of Jesus himself, but does not render him speechless if authentic sayings are still accessible in the tradition. Bultmann, moreover, has fostered such helpful suggestions in the idea of history itself that his insistence on the unimportance for Christian thought of the history of Jesus is not so categorical as it initially sounds.

We mention these things to make clear the formidable obstacles that must be faced if one proposes to discuss the political ideas of Jesus. Just as it was judged at an earlier time that we cannot for want of scientific, clinical evidence make a psychiatric study of Jesus, it will be judged by many that a political biography is equally impossible. In 1929–30, however, Robert Eisler sought to explain Jesus along political lines. In 1967, S. G. F. Brandon undertook the same task in *Jesus and the Zealots*. Since Brandon's work inspired a number of writers (as in the case of Colin Morris) to reassess the issue of violence in the life of Jesus, it is necessary to place his argument under observation. We proceed to that here, with special reference to Matthew.

The Brandon Thesis

Jesus was crucified under Pilate as an insurrectionist (Mark 15:26; see synoptic parallels). The Barabbas story, unattested in Roman law of the period, is not historical. Its motive is to show Pilate in a favorable light by placing direct blame on the Jewish leaders for the death of Jesus. Thus Mark is an apology (defense) addressed to Roman Christians to promote cordial relations between Christianity and Rome by obscuring Jesus' kinship with the Jewish freedom fighters, the Zealots. Mark 3:18 calls Simon the "Cananaean." This Aramaic name is employed by Mark to obscure the fact that Jesus enlisted Zealots among his disciples, since Luke 6:15 shows that Cananaean means Zealot. The tribute saying in Mark 12:17 par., when read correctly, reflects Zealot repudiation of Roman tax rights. The saying on cross-bearing (Matt. 10:38 par.) derives from the Zealots and reflects the political fate (i.e., death) that their followers expected. The entry of Jesus into Jerusalem and the cleansing of the temple clearly demonstrate a political-messianic movement, employing violent means if need be, a fact also suggested by the armed confrontation in the garden of Gethsemane (Mark 14:43–50 par). The miraculous splitting of the temple curtain (Mark 15:38 par.) epitomizes Mark's negative judgment on Jewish culture and religion, while the confession of the centurion (Mark 15:39 par.) puts Rome in a favored light. Jewish Christians loyally perished in the final defense of Jerusalem and did not, as some report, flee to Pella. Though Matthew is a Jewish Christian Gospel, it was written in Alexandria (not Syria) and extensively obscured, even more than Mark, Jesus' patriotic devotion to Israel's cause. Luke and John show the same tendency, further obscuring the historical character of Jesus and Jewish Christianity, which succumbed before the spiritualizing and universalizing gospel preached by Paul.

Further details of Brandon's idea will be given as the discussion proceeds. Using mainly the evidence supplied by the historian Josephus, Brandon has carefully and helpfully expounded first-century conditions in Palestine and the growth of the Jewish revolt. His thesis has been further elaborated in *The Fall of Jerusalem and the Christian Church* (1957) and *The Trial of Jesus of Nazareth* (1968), as well as in a number of scholarly articles.

It is essential to the understanding of Brandon's hypotheses to explain their kinship to the earlier work of Eisler.

Eisler, Brandon, and the Slavonic Josephus

In the index of *Jesus and the Zealots* there are no less than
sixty-seven references to Eisler's *Messiah Jesus* or its German
counterpart. Careful reading of these references shows considerable, though not invariable, concurrence. Those acquainted with
the works of both scholars are so struck by the panoramic similarity between them, however, that it will be helpful to specifically
illustrate it here.

Brandon repeatedly[3] treats the article before "insurrection"
in Mark 15:7 as a factual reference to a historical event, even
though he regards the Barabbas amnesty offered by Pilate as
wholly fictitious, arising from Mark's pro-Roman tendency.[4] He
further maintains that Jesus' action in cleansing the temple "coincided" with this Zealot insurrection and that "it would be reasonable to suppose" the two events were connected (i.e., the
temple cleansing and the Zealot uprising involving Barabbas).[5]
In this context, Brandon refers in a footnote to Eisler, who narrates how Jesus and the disciples seized the temple and were
driven out by the Romans.[6] To bolster this interpretation, Eisler
wrenches Luke 13:1 from its own context and brings it in to fill
out the consequence of this insurgency, i.e., a violent repression
by Pilate. In the "Wonderworker" passage from the Slavonic
Josephus (quoted below), one finds the text from which Eisler
built this patchwork quilt of political exegesis. Recognizing the
the broadspread repudiation which Eisler's work has experienced,
Brandon uses a guarded form of reference to Eisler, but cannot
erase the impression that the two approaches are intimately kin.

Eisler's two-volume work in German, completed in 1930, bore
the Greek title *IESOUS BASILEUS OU BASILEUSAS*, which
means "Jesus the king that didn't reign." The phrase comes from

an Old Russian version of *The Jewish War* ascribed to Josephus and referred to variously as the Slavonic (or Slavic) Josephus, or *Halosis*, Greek for "destruction" (of Jerusalem). In 1906 Alexander Berendts first published in German the passages from the Slavonic Josephus that deal with John the Baptist, the "Wonder-worker" (Jesus), and Christian origins—materials not heretofore known from manuscripts of Josephus.[7] Though he posited an intermediary translation in Greek, Berendts held that the new materials went back ultimately to an original Aramaic version of the *War* referred to by Josephus himself when he wrote (*War*, 1:1): "I . . . propose to provide the subjects of the Roman Empire with a narrative of the facts, by translating into Greek the account which *I previously composed in my own vernacular tongue* and sent to the barbarians in the interior" [italics added].

For our considerations, the most important of the Slavonic additions is the one on the "Wonder-Worker" quoted below. The parenthetical words are explanatory additions by the translator. The bracketed words are those that Eisler rejected as Christian interpolations.

The Ministry, Trial and Crucifixion of "the Wonder-Worker" (Jesus)

At that time there appeared a man, if it is permissible to call him a man. His nature [and form] were human, but his appearance (was something more than (that) of a man, [notwithstanding his works were divine]. He worked miracles wonderful and mighty. [Therefore it is impossible for me to call him a man;] but again, if I look at the nature which he shared with all, I will not call him an angel. And everything whatsoever he wrought through an invisible power, he wrought by word and command. Some said of him, "Our first lawgiver is risen from the dead and hath performed many healings and arts," while others thought that he was sent from God. Howbeit in many things he disobeyed the Law and kept not the Sabbath according to (our) fathers' customs. Yet, on the other hand, he did nothing shameful; nor (did he do anything) with aid of hands, but by word alone did he provide everything.

And many of the multitude followed after him and hearkened to his teaching; and many souls were in commotion, thinking that thereby the

Jewish tribes might free themselves from Roman hands. Now it was his custom in general to sojourn over against the city upon the Mount of Olives; and there, too, he bestowed his healings upon the people.

And there assembled unto him of ministers one hundred and fifty, and a multitude of the people. Now when they saw his power, that he accomplished whatsoever he would by (a) word, and when they had made known to him their will, that he should enter into the city and cut down the Roman troops and Pilate and rule over us, he disdained us not.

And when thereafter knowledge of it came to the Jewish leaders, they assembled together with the high-priests and spake: "We are powerless and (too) weak to withstand the Romans. Seeing, moreover, that the bow is bent, we will go and communicate to Pilate what we have heard, and we shall be clear of trouble, lest he hear it from others, and we be robbed of our substance, and ourselves slaughtered and our children scattered." And they went and communicated (it) to Pilate. And he sent and had many of the multitude slain. And he had that Wonder-worker brought up, and after instituting an inquiry concerning him he pronounced judgement: "He is [a benefactor, not] a malefactor, [nor] a rebel, [nor]covetous of kingship. [And he let him go; for he had healed his dying wife.]

[And he went to his wonted place and did his wonted works. And when more people again assembled round him, he glorified himself through his actions more than all. The teachers of the Law were overcome with envy, and gave thirty talents to Pilate, in order that he should put him to death. And he took (it) and gave them liberty to execute their will themselves.] And they laid hands on him and crucified him contrary to the Law of (their) fathers.[8]

This passage is bristling with critical difficulties. "He disdained us not" at the end of the third paragraph is a crucial phrase, because it indicates Jesus' willingness to lead the uprising (cf. Mark 15:7). But another text reads at this point, "he heeded us not," which gives the passage quite a different sense. If, moreover, the interpreter is permitted to expunge from a manuscript whatever appears extraneous to him on grounds of content, the final product may be expected to say nearly anything he wishes.

Brandon holds that the poor reception accorded Eisler's publication was due to the shock it gave to orthodox belief.[9] This opinion obscures the fact, however, that eminent scholars—Jewish, Christian, and agnostic—repudiated the *Halosis* long before Eisler wrote. Emil Schürer, the renowned Jewish historian, ascribed the *Halosis* to a forger of the Byzantine era (twelfth century). He also scored the logic of Berendts when he held that the texts *must* derive from Josephus since the veneration of Jesus is greater than a Jewish forgery would permit, yet insufficient to suspect a Christian one.[10] In 1928 another well-known Jewish scholar, Solomon Zeitlin, traveled to Russia to see the manuscripts, concluding that no Aramaic could underlie them because the names they contain are not Hebrew by derivation but Syro-Macedonian.[11]

After the publication of Eisler's work, scholars once again repudiated the texts on which his theory was based. J. M. Creed, for example, reiterated the question that others had already raised: "if a writer so well known and so widely read as Josephus had written these remarkable accounts of John the Baptist and Jesus Christ, and if these were present in any text of the Jewish War current during the early centuries, how does it come about that ante-Nicene Christian literature knows nothing about them?"[12] Still Brandon sought to defend Eisler (and the *Halosis*) by appealing to an article by Arie Rubinstein.[13] One is hardly convinced by this when one sees that Rubinstein's essay 1) denies that the texts go back to a Semitic original, 2) acknowledges, with Schürer, the twelfth-century origin of the material, and 3) omits from discussion the passage on the "Wonderworker," the very one that Eisler exploits. In respect to these disputed "additions" to the standard Josephan text, Rubinstein defers to the work of J. W. Jack, whose opinion is that the Byzantine forerunner of the *Halosis* was composed not earlier than the eleventh century by an author who seems to have been a converted Jew or a Christian.[14] This author's writing was done "with the object of giving a Christian version of Josephus' history of the War, and accordingly it contained many Christian interpolations." Jack's

contribution swelled the tide of critical opinion that stood against
the authenticity of the Slavic version. More recently, W. Foerster
summarized the consensus of scholarly judgment in this fashion:
"Middle-age Old Russian manuscripts offer a text which is often
deviate. Eisler traced this back to Josephus himself and from it
inferred a political-messianic life of Jesus. This thesis, with
reason, became generally rejected, as also Eisler's high opinion of
the Old Russian text altogether."[15]

By discussing Eisler's treatment of "taking up the cross" in
Matthew 10:38, further comparison between his position and that
of Brandon is possible. Eisler expounds the notion that the
Rechabites, a group of anti-Baal reformists instituted in the time
of Elijah and Elisha (cf. 2 Kings 10:15–17), marked themselves
with a cross sign on the forehead (cf. Ezek. 9:4) as a token of
their common commitment.[16] By New Testament times they had
evolved into a sect of homeless, nonviolent pietists, followers first
of John the Baptist, then of Jesus. Taking up the cross was thus
an allusion to the cross sign of the Rechabite sect.

Brandon drops the Rechabite argument, for which he is to
be commended, but appeals to Adolf Schlatter and Martin Hengel
for the repeated assertion that taking up the cross was an in-
itiatory watchword borrowed from the Zealots.[17] (Hengel actually depends on Schlatter for this suggestion.)

Unfortunately for Brandon's cause, Hengel wrote in the
Journal of Semitic Studies one of the severest criticisms of *Jesus
and the Zealots* yet to appear, despite the fact that Brandon frequently draws upon Hengel's own book, *Die Zeloten* (1961), to
develop his argument.[18] Hengel by no means substantiates the
inferences that Brandon places on his allusion to "taking up
the cross."

Schlatter is not present to discuss what political implications
he might have attached to his brief references to this topic, but
we can deduce his response without difficulty. Schlatter held to
the priority of Matthew, espoused a conservative position on the
historicity of the Jesus traditions preserved in that Gospel, and

repeatedly found in Matthew an anti-Zealot polemic.[19] Thus it can be said with virtual certitude that he did not intend his remark on Matthew 10:38 to perform the work placed on it in the Brandon hypothesis.

Thus far, Eisler does not seem to have determined Brandon's approach. But we must not draw a hasty conclusion from this. In the Sermon on the Mount, Eisler finds authentic teaching of Jesus directed against the Zealot cause of armed insurgency.[20] Jesus' teaching against retaliation (Matthew 5:38–42), he held, came from the Rechabites.[21] How then, on Eisler's terms, is the shift to violence which came in the attack on Jerusalem in the triumphal entry to be explained? It came about by an increasing awareness on Jesus' part that a divine intervention would result only through some more decisive action on his part.[22] So Jesus broke, possibly under the influence of Zealots in his company of followers, and was driven "forward on the fatal road" of violence. Indeed, the famous pacifist text of Matthew 26:52 ("Put your sword back into its place; for all who take the sword will perish by the sword") echoes Jesus' realization that *he himself,* having now resorted to the sword, will be brought under its edge, i.e., in his crucifixion, which will effect the divine intervention.[23]

Brandon, in contrast, ascribes to Jesus no such break with (Rechabite) nonviolence as that Eisler proposes. Discerning, with Eisler, the gross impediments that Matthew—not only in the Gethsemane eposide of the sword, but particularly in the Sermon on the Mount with its Beatitudes, its radical, anti-Zealot rejection of retaliation, and its injunction on the love of enemies—erects against the theory of Jesus' political messianism, he must *exceed the revisions attempted by Eisler* and propose a setting for Matthew that eliminates any possible connection between these aspects of Matthew and the historical Jesus.[24] We conjecture from this that Brandon's ostensible independence from Eisler represents not a break with but an actual refinement of the Eisler hypothesis.

Brandon discreetly assigns the discussion of the *Halosis* to an appendix of *Jesus and the Zealots*. This removal of it from central prominence is indeed a requirement impelled by the canons of historical criticism, but it also enlarges the role that must be played by arguments from silence and inventive conjecture. What Maurice Goguel wrote, then, in 1929 about Eisler's method is entirely apposite to that of Brandon:

The first virtue of the historian ought to remain his submissiveness to the texts. It is necessary to protect himself from forcing them to say what he wants them to say. His second virtue, which is in sum only another form of the first, ought to be to challenge hypotheses. Surely history cannot do without conjectures entirely, but it ought to make only the minimum which is necessary to unite the given elements within the text, and it should not hazard any which contradict the positive indications of the text, or even that which would not be, in some measure, the extension of them.[25]

More recently, Hans Jonas has commented on the centrality of language (i.e., written materials) in historical understanding.[26] Unlike present discourse, "the past has no vocal chords." It cannot add correctives, but remains defenseless. Thus fidelity in the hearing is mandatory.

Jewish Christians and the Flight to Pella

It would appear on the surface of the matter that an ancient allusion or two to the flight of Jewish Christians from Jerusalem to Pella (east of the Jordan river about 15 miles south of the Sea of Galilee) in connection with the Jewish war of A.D. 66–70 would have nothing to do with the political understanding of Jesus. Eisler, in fact, accepts the Pella tradition. Brandon rejects it. We must discover why.

Eusebius tells about the migration in his *Ecclesiastical History*:

"Moreover, the people of the church at Jerusalem, in accordance with a certain oracle that was vouchsafed by way of revelation to approved men there, had been commanded to depart from the city before the war, and to inhabit a certain city of Peraea. They called it Pella."[27] Eusebius died in A.D. 340. There are also fifth-century references to the Pella flight in the writings of Epiphanius. Regarding the phrase, "depart from the city before the war," in the above quotation, Brandon translates, "an oracle, given by revelation to men approved before the war, to depart from the city. . . ."[28] As Walter Wink has pointed out, Brandon's translation is erroneous in making "before the war" modify "approved" instead of "depart from the city."[29] Wink may also be correct in branding this a "patently tendentious" translation in light of the following.

Brandon wishes to establish that there was no fitting time when the Jewish Christians could have gone to Pella. Josephus narrates (*War*, 2:458) that Pella was sacked by the Jews in retaliation for a massacre experienced by Jews in Caesarea. This was in A.D. 66, when revolutionary tensions and repressive moves by the Romans were on the rise. Brandon conjectures that if the Jerusalem Christians had gone there before this reprisal, they would have perished in it. If they had gone after it, they would have been caught by Vespasian's exterminating campaign in that area in A.D. 68, also narrated by Josephus (*War*, 4:413–39). When Jerusalem was put under siege, moreover, there was manifestly no chance of their escape. So no proper time is to be found to substantiate the Pella story. It is also to be ruled out (so Brandon says) on the ground that Eusebius is anxious in his account to depict the fall of Jerusalem as a divine judgment on an impenitent Judaism, a judgment that can transpire only after the righteous remnant (i.e., the Jewish Christians) have made their exit.

Brandon's conjectures in this regard affect a certitude that historical judgment cannot permit. Why is it to be presumed, for example, that Jewish marauders would have killed fellow Jews from

Jerusalem who had settled in Pella? Though Josephus tells of Vespasian's conquest of Perea, Pella itself is not specifically mentioned in that part of the *War*. Josephus also notes, as Brandon concedes, that a number of Sicarii survived the siege of Jerusalem and fled to Egypt (*War*, 7:410), and Brandon himself espouses the view that some Jewish Christians endured the holocaust and also found their way to Alexandria:

Now, there is reason for thinking that, although the Mother Church of Jerusalem disappeared, a significant number of Jewish Christians did escape from war-devastated Judea and found refuge in Egypt, particularly in Alexandria. The events would, accordingly, have made the church in Alexandria the chief surviving center of Jewish Christianity.[30]

Since conjectural arguments are thus so insubstantial, we are compelled to seek further to explain the aversion for the Pella tradition.

In his treatment of Jesus and the Zealots, Brandon wishes to show that Jesus was one with the revolutionary sect in the cause of patriotic nationalism. He makes this point so emphatically that even so distinguished a Jewish scholar as Samuel Sandmel ascribes to Brandon the view that Jesus himself was a Zealot, though Brandon does not literally express himself so.[31] Since, however, Jesus, Zealots, and early Jerusalem Christians were one in militant patriotic fervor, it is obvious to Brandon that Jerusalem Christians of the first church loyally defended the city to the end against Roman overthrow, and perished with it. Flight to Pella before or even during the war, before or after the Jerusalem siege, would have been unthinkably disloyal.

Countering the tendentious revision of Brandon on this point, W. D. Davies has commented on Pella as follows:

. . . they left the city for refuge in Pella probably in A.D. 68. The number of the Christians who left was probably small, otherwise they would not have been allowed to go. There is nothing to suggest that it was detachment from the national aspirations of their people after the flesh nor indifference to the fate of Jerusalem that induced them to depart, naturally as their conduct was so construed by Jewry. What is clear is that they rejected the extreme militarism of the Zealots and obeyed what they regarded as the will of God.[32]

H. J. Schoeps, perhaps the most eminent existing authority on early Jewish Christianity, has stated the case more emphatically than Davies in a review of the first edition of Brandon's *Fall of Jerusalem*:

It seems to me, just because of the pacifist outlook on life which I have shown to be theirs, that in politics they were typical pietists. That is also the reason why the Jewish Christians withdrew to Transjordan soon after the outbreak of the War of Liberation of 66, thus snapping their fingers at national solidarity, just as the returned immigrants in the Bar Kochba rising of 135 also stood aside, according to the evidence of Orosius (vii. 3), and preferred to let themselves be killed by their compatriots (Justin, *Apology*, i, 35, 5–6). I must say: remarkable nationalists![33]

Hence it is difficult to avoid the conclusion that the flight to Pella is negated in *Jesus and the Zealots* because it presents Jewish Christians as opposed to the Zealot ideal and weakens the case for political violence ascribed to Jesus and the earliest disciples.

Since, as noted above, Brandon does assert that some Jewish Christians managed to find both a time and a means for escape to Alexandria, we must now observe how and why this assertion is related to his discussion of the origin of the Gospel of Matthew.

The Provenance of Matthew

Brandon holds that Matthew was written at Alexandria.[34] His arguments in this regard may be summarized as follows. The

story of the Alexandrian Apollos in Acts 18:24–28 is typological
in the sense that the author of Acts, a devotee of Pauline Chris-
tianity, wishes to rebut in the figure of Apollos the Petrine
Christianity of Alexandria. Peter, who strangely disappears after
Acts 12:17, went to Alexandria where he presided over the Jewish
Christian community. The centrality of Peter in Matthew demonstrates its Alexandrian provenance. The flight to Egypt in
Matthew 2:13–15 is also the evangelist's esoteric way of showing
Matthew's connection with Egypt. Early documents associated
with Egypt (i.e., Barnabas, 2 Clement, and the Gospel of Thomas)
show close knowledge of Matthew. Cumulatively, these factors
indicate that the first Gospel did not derive from somewhere in
Syria, as frequently assumed, but from Egypt.

This brings us to the issue of the peculiar political stamp
of Matthew. As Stendahl declares, Matthew "is readily described
as the Gospel which has the strongest Jewish flavour."[35] This
standard view is also shared by Brandon. But now comes the
paradox: How can the peaceableness of Jesus in Matthew, even
more pronounced than that in Mark, be reconciled with the
militant nationalism found (by Brandon) among the Jewish
Christians? The solution is that Alexandrian Jewish Christianity,
smarting from the terrific impact of Jerusalem's fall and seeing
the prudence of avoiding further Roman reprisals, plays the
revisionist game of Mark with even greater thoroughness. Thus
the real sense of the saying against the sword in Matthew 26:52
is that it reminds the readers of that folly by which early Christians had made "common cause with their fellow-Jews in the
struggle to redeem Israel from its servitude to the heathen."[36]

We shall now proceed to show that arguments for the
Alexandrian origin of Matthew are not convincing. Then we
must point out what the consequences of a more correct view of
Matthew would be.

That Apollos serves as an epynomic figure for Alexandrian
Christianity has also been maintained by Arnold Ehrhardt, fol-

lowing Walter Bauer.[37] But Brandon makes too much of this. It is an oversimplification to say that Jerusalem Christianity, with its strongly ethnic and political christology, yielded to the Pauline spiritualizations about the cross as the sin-remitting climax of the church's preachment.[38] When Paul narrates (1 Cor. 15:3) what he already inherits in Christian tradition, it contains the affirmation that "Christ died for our sins in accordance with the scriptures." This was not invented but inherited by Paul.

In his 1950 discussion of "Tübingen Vindicated?" Brandon sought to refurbish the well-worn Hegelian dialectic of a Jewish (Petrine) Christianity polarized with a Gentile (Pauline) Christainity, the thesis and antithesis that synthesized in early Catholicism.[39] Discussing the factions at Corinth, to which Brandon also appeals for his Peter/Paul scheme, Conzelmann has more recently concluded that we are not faced with a conflict between Jewish and Gentile Christianity in 1 Corinthians 1–4.[40] Paul does not fight the Peter party and "The assumption that the Peter-people reject Paul is groundless."[41] Of James (early head of the Jerusalem church) and Paul, Schmithals has said that "theological differences between Paul and James were not significant enough to separate the churches."[42] Acts, moreover, is an improper resource out of which to form a historical typology for either Petrine or Pauline christological ideals, since current opinion has it that the author of Acts wrote from the perspective of his own, later time, lacking intimate, acquaintance with essential ideas of Paul.[43]

Acts 12:17 tells absolutely nothing about the destination of Peter. The Alexandrian church named Mark as its patron saint and founder. It is difficult to explain this tradition, however legendary it probably is, if Peter (and Matthew) were closely connected with the Alexandrian church at its beginning.

Brandon is aware of W. D. Davies's treatment of the flight to Egypt paradigm in Matthew 2:13–15.[44] Davies and others carefully demonstrate that this midrashic tale represents a piece of haggadah on the idea of Hosea 11:1, "Out of Egypt I called my son," cited in Matthew 2:15. This Exodus motif accords well with the Jewish-Christian style of Matthew and is further attested by the echo of Exodus 4:19 ("All the men who were seeking your life are dead") in Matthew 2:20, "those who sought the child's life are dead" (even though it is only Herod who had died!). In other words, Matthew's usual proclivity to christianize familiar themes of Jewish tradition entirely satisfies the ideological aura of Matthew 2:13-15 without any appeal to the Alexandrian provenance of Matthew.

As to the Matthaean references in Barnabas, 2 Clement, and the Gospel of Thomas, this may be the most counterproductive part of the argument. In connection with the provenance of Mark, Brandon appeals in another context to B. W. Bacon's *Is Mark a Roman Gospel?*. Discussing the Apostolic Fathers, Bacon points out that none of them, except possibly Hermas, shows preference for Mark. Then he adds: "Predilection, as soon as traceable in the Fathers, is always in favor of Matthew."[45] This predilection was due to the supposed apostolic authorship of Matthew, its imposing length and schematic organization, and the widespread early opinion that it was the first Gospel written. Bertil Gärtner does grant that "The Gospel of Thomas on a few occasions makes use of distinctly Matthaean material (e.g., in logia 76 and 109), and in a number of sayings approximates more closely to the Matthaean version. . . ."[46] This same sentence ends, however: "but in the majority of cases it is Luke which predominates." Was Luke also written in Alexandria? Right in the bosom of Petrine Christianity? Helmut Koester adds to this: "Luke 11:27–12:56 is paralleled by no less than thirteen sayings in the Gospel of Thomas; seven of these have parallels only in Luke."[47]

It has been argued, moreover, by Koester, Quispel, A. F. J. Klijn, and others that the sayings of the Gospel of Thomas ultimately derive from the city of Edessa in East Syria.[48] The

debate over this position is not yet settled, but it is patently un-
wise at this stage to connect Matthew with Thomas so as to locate
Matthew in Alexandria when, in fact, the argument may carry us
back to Syria again!

To what point, then, has this discussion brought us? Evidence
reviewed indicates that we cannot reasonably join Matthaean
Christianity to Alexandria and thus polarize it with Pauline
Christianity. If Jewish Christians did not fade into oblivion with
the events of A.D. 70 but escaped the city and carried away traditions of the early Jerusalem church, it is logical to conclude that
Matthew, despite distinct Hellenistic features as well, retains
christological and ethical ideas in direct descent from the Palestinian matrix in which these ideas were nurtured. If this is so,
should we not grant that Matthew, instead of representing a 180-
degree shift from the Zealot-inclined, patriotic Jesus of history,
actually reflected in his peaceable Christ the very christology
that Jerusalem Christians believed? The burden of proof would
still seem to lie with those who deny this conclusion. We must
take one further look at Matthew, however, to broaden the base
of our observation.

Matthew's Temptation Story

The event of Jerusalem's fall in A.D. 70 and the collapse of
the Zealot resistance are integral to Brandon's conception of the
writing of Matthew and Mark, integral, indeed, to the shaping of
the whole of early Christian belief. The collapse of Zealotism and
the necessary accomodation to Roman rule that followed there-
upon gave to the Gospel writers, it is held, the peculiar political
focus that enabled them to erase, except for a few hints here and
there, Jesus' complicity in the cause of violent Jewish nationalism.

With regard to Matthew's story of the temptation (4:1–11), the sum of our argument is this: The final composition of Matthew in A.D. 80 or 85 should not eclipse the fact that Matthew employs sources that precede this by several decades. Indeed, in the Q source, that source common to Matthew and Luke in addition to their other common source Mark,[49] we meet traditions that unmistakably emanate from a time prior to the fall of Jerusalem, no matter how late in the first century Matthew may write. If, finally, it becomes clear that the pacific Christ appears in the Q source, it is impossible to explain it as an editorial tendency compelled by politics subsequent to A.D. 70.

Matthew 4:1–11 and Luke 4:1–13 build the temptation story in language almost identical.[50] Thus we encounter here the Q source. Brandon recognizes this.[51] Yet his analysis of the story raises serious methodological objections.

First, he presupposes that "Mark knew of a Temptation tradition" but ignored it for the sake of his own apologetical concerns.[52] Since there is no other temptation (besides Mark's) at stake except the one common to Matthew and Luke, Brandon's ambiguous phraseology refers of necessity to the familiar three-fold temptation of Q. But Mark discloses no knowledge of this whatever. Lohmeyer appropriately comments:

Not a word is said in Mk about the content of the temptation, and this silence is still more striking in view of the scribal dialogue in [the temptation story of] Mt and Lk. One cannot give the explanation that Mk has assumed a·more complete knowledge of the matter among his hearers and thus intentionally abbreviated the story, for his words bear a linguistic garb which is different from that of the sayings source. He follows therefore another tradition which knows only the fact of the temptation. . . .[53] (Bracketed words added.)

With this inadmissable premise, Brandon proceeds to connect the threefold temptation with the Beelzebul charge in Mark 3:22.[54] The "Pharisees" who lodged the Beelzebul charge must have been that quietist and pacifist section of the party that abstained from political activity. And how does one get from the "scribes" in Mark 3:22 to these "Pharisees"? By taking them from the parallel to Mark 3:22 that is found in Matthew 12:24. Commenting, however, on the redactionary character of the various adversaries employed in the tradition, Bultmann has pointed out that Luke's Beelzebul incident (Luke 11:15) has merely "some of them."[55] He further reflects that since Luke derives "some of them" from the Q source, both scribes (Mark) and Pharisees (Matthew) are editorial. Hence Brandon's historicizing of "Pharisees" is groundless, even if he were granted the unusual liberty of importing it into Mark from Matthew.

But what does this have to do with the temptation story in Matthew? Offended at Jesus' attack on the temple banking system (Mark 11:15-19 par), these quietist Pharisees were countering the "Messianic claims of Jesus with the charge that Jesus had been inspired by Satan to seek world-empire and had caused a political crisis in Jerusalem, which resulted in his death. . . ."[56] To nullify this charge of the Pharisees, the Jewish Christians coined the threefold temptation as a vehicle for showing that Jesus had nothing to do with conquest and empire. Hence Mark, knowing the origin of the story, thought it best to ignore it "in the interests of his own apologetical theme."

These tortuous exegetical maneuvers must lay bare the fact that in the temptation story are elements that threaten the most vital parts of his whole hypothesis.

Bultmann traces the narrative to the earliest stratum of Gospel history: "On the basis of its form, the Temptation story in Q belongs to the sphere of the Palestinian Tradition which indeed also indicates its belonging to Q."[57] He further emphasizes that the story is built on Jewish Christian ideas: "The story of the Temptation . . . is fashioned in the spirit of Judaistic Christianity. . . ."[58] Brandon's recognition of these positions leads his theory into a dead end. Jewish Christianity must consistently exemplify the most militant kind of anti-Roman nationalism, particularly in the period prior to A.D. 70, when armed resistance had not yet proven itself a vain hope. Yet, in this distinctive piece of Jewish Christian thought about Jesus, his pacific designs are very boldly stated.

The messianic consciousness of Jesus himself is not at stake in this context.[59] What is at stake in the temptation legend is how the earliest Christians thought about Jesus' messiahship. Their reflections were not philosophical speculations designed for the Chalcedonian language of the fifth century, but existential and ethical probings in which they sought the definition of their own calling in the world.

Schlatter, with notable perspicacity, drew out the ethical import of Matthew 4:1–11 in this manner: "It is however correct that with the godliness which is here described as the possession of Jesus, the popular messianic ideas are set aside. Whether they were colored by Zealotic, Pharisaic, or Sadducean ideas, they all had other goals than the ones which are derived in this case from God's communion with Jesus."[60] Schlatter's comprehension of the material is attested in the history of exegesis from the earliest time forward. Cullmann more recently followed customary views in interpreting the third temptation (i.e., conquest of earthly kingdoms) as an expression of anti-Zealot ideas in line with Jesus' rejection of Peter's notion of messiahship in Matthew 16:21–23, and the repudiation of the sword in the Gethsemane episode of Matthew 26:52–53.[61] With modest variations, this is the exposition developed earlier by Stendahl.[62] We cannot say, of course, that texts like Matthew 5:9, 5:41, or 26:52 belong to Q.[63] What we do assert is that these and similar texts have clear ethical antecedents in Q and cannot, therefore, be explained as though the two groups of material mirror opposite poles of political development.

To recapitulate, what we encounter in the temptation narrative is material exhibiting christological ideas of the Palestinian (not Alexandrine), Judaic Christian church from a time well antecedent to the political-military disaster of A.D. 70. With its negative implications for political intrigue and military conquest, it cannot be made to serve a view of Jewish Christianity that makes it a handmaiden of Zealotic nationalism. While it can be conceded to Brandon that Matthew's portrait of Christ accentuates the pacific lineaments already drawn by Mark, the ingredients of that portrait predate Mark and the alleged political motivations that gave it birth.

Conclusion

To retain a contemporary consciousness in these deliberations, we return for a moment to a statement about *Jesus and the Zealots* made by Colin Morris: "it is the standard text for any Christian trying to make sense of the revolutions of our time, even though the Professor does not stray by so much as a page out of the world of Jesus' time."[64]

The impression that Brandon confines himself to first-century issues is unwarranted. On pages 23 through 25 of *Jesus and the Zealots*, he asserts that Christian scholars have failed in general to discern the political facts of Jesus' life because the concept of the Divine Savior has lent a nonhistorical or nonpolitical air to New Testament research. In Britain, further, an instinctive rejection of political murder and sabotage has operated because they signify a threat to western capitalism, making the Zealot cause on the very face of it repugnant. During World War II, however, a new awareness of the courage and heroism of resistance groups in Nazi-occupied lands emerged.[65] This has opened new interest in the Zealots and the political aspects of Jesus.

This same idea is expressed in Brandon's *Trial of Jesus*, with the addition of reference to the cause of contemporary Israel:

The Second World War, when "resistance" groups in many lands struggled fiercely, using guerilla tactics often involving assassination and murder, against the occupying Nazi forces, induced willingness to look at the ancient Zealots with a new and sympathetic insight. This new atmosphere also coincided with the establishment of the new state of Israel against what seemed in 1948 to be impossible odds. In their dedicated struggle, the Israelis found inspiration in the example of those Zealots who, in the year 73 at Masada, fought to the bitter end, preferring suicide to surrender to the Romans. The excavation of this great fortress on the shores of the Dead Sea was undertaken by the Israeli government in 1963 not only as a piece of archaeological research, but as a gesture of national faith: the results have been to demonstrate both the heroism and the essentially religious character of Zealotism.[66]

No one who has heard the distinguished Israeli archaeologist Yigael Yadin unfold the fascinating story of the excavation of Masada with its crowning dedicatory ceremony built around the theme, "Masada shall not fall again," can doubt that even the science of archaeology flies its distinct political banners.[67]

But that is just where the ethical issue erupts.

In the wake of Israel's advances since 1945 we have witnessed another blend of national devotion and religious enthusiasm among the Arabic communities of the Middle East and in the numerous resistance groups within and without Palestine. Dr. George Habash, head of the Popular Front for the Liberation of Palestine, has spoken movingly of the displacement that Palestinian people suffered when the Israelis came to Lydda in 1967:

Then it was 1967 and they came to Lydda and . . . I don't know how to explain this . . . what this still means for us not to have a home, not to have a nation or anyone who cares. . . . They forced us to flee. It is a picture that haunts me and that I'll never forget. Thirty thousand human beings walking, weeping . . . screaming in terror . . . women with babies in their arms and children tugging at their skirts . . . and

the Israeli soldiers pushing them on with their guns. Some people fell by
the wayside, some never got up again. It was terrible. One thinks: this
isn't life, this isn't human. . . . One must change the world, do something,
kill if necessary, even at the risk of becoming inhuman in our turn. . . .[68]

The Palestinian nationalists did something. They claimed responsibility for the school bus bombing of May 22, 1970, near the
Lebanese border in which eleven were killed and twenty-one
wounded, most of them children.[69] By several plane hijackings
in 1970 and warfare in Jordan, the PFLP achieved further international fame as they paid allegiance to their heroic vow: Palestine for the Palestinians.

One should not doubt, as Brandon correctly emphasizes, that
Josephus exhibits his own *Tendenzen*.[70] If the Zealots had succeeded, Josephus would not have written the words that close
this chapter. The issue being raised in this book, however, is
whether there is not something in the problem of violence that
transcends the criterion of success. The Maccabees succeeded.
But they also failed. We must, then, allow to Josephus a measure
of descriptive accuracy when he summarized the impact of the
Zealot ideal:

They sowed the seed from which sprang strife between factions and the
slaughter of fellow citizens. Some were slain in civil strife, for these
men madly had recourse to butchery of each other and of themselves from
a longing not to be outdone by their opponents; others were slain by the
enemy in war. Then came famine, reserved to exhibit the last degree of
shamelessness, followed by the storming and razing of cities until at last
the very temple of God was ravaged by the enemy's fire through this
revolt. . . . In this case certainly, Judas and Saddok started among us an
intrusive fourth school of philosophy; and when they had won an abundance of devotees, they filled the whole body politic immediately with
tumult, also planting the seeds of those troubles which subsequently
overtook it, all because of the novelty of this hitherto unknown philosophy that I shall now describe. My reason for giving this brief account
of it is chiefly that the zeal which Judas and Saddok inspired in the
younger element meant the ruin of our cause.[71]

III. MARK'S
"POLITICAL APOLOGY"

In the foregoing chapter, we have attempted to show that in one of the two primary Gospel sources, Q, there are solid reasons for concluding that the pacific Christ was known in the tradition prior to the fall of Jerusalem, as early as A.D. 50. We turn now to Mark, the second major source. By examining certain passages in Mark, we seek to determine whether they disclose a tendentious rapprochment between Christianity and Rome, a rapprochment that falsified the closeness of Jesus to Jewish nationalism and set the style for an early Christian anti-Semitism. As in our examination of Matthew, we shall see in some instances that the evidence decisively excludes Mark's supposed "political apology." In other, less decisive cases, the evidence can yield this political tendency only when other conclusions equally suggested by the text are overridden. We begin with an illustration from this latter category.

The Veil of the Temple
Mark 15:38–39 (= Matt. 27:51–54 = Luke 23:45–47)

Brandon found in the splitting of the veil of the temple (Mark 15:38) an allusion to the Flavian triumph celebrated in Rome in A.D. 71.[1] The temple curtain on this occasion was paraded

44

through the streets of Rome along with other trophies of the victory, so when Mark referred to the veil, Roman readers would have had visual contact with it. Its prodigious rending in Mark 15:38 would have meant to them the judgment of God upon Judaism just as the confession of the Roman centurion in verse 39 would have implied divine favor on Rome. These verses thus disclose both the occasion and purpose of Mark's writing:

It was an apologetic designed to cope with the dangerous and perplexing situation in which the Christian community at Rome was placed by the Jewish revolt and the publicity given to it at the Flavian triumph. Mark wrote his Gospel with a twofold intent: to explain away the problem of the Roman execution of Jesus and present him as loyal to Rome; and to show that Jesus, though born a Jew, had no essential connection with the Jewish people and their religion, and that a Gentile was the first to preceive this truth, to which the Jews were blind, that Jesus was the Son of God.[2]

Now it cannot be disputed that in the history of Christianity this passage was so understood. H. J. Schoeps has drawn attention to this view in connection with the apocryphal Gospel According to the Hebrews.[3] But the issue has to do with Mark's meaning, not those who commented on what he wrote. A passage in the Slavonic Josephus (following *War*, 5:214) coincides with Brandon's interpretation: "This curtain was before this generation entire, because the people were pious; but now it was grevious to see, for it was suddenly rent from the top to the bottom, when they through bribery delivered to death the benefactor of men and him who from his actions was no man."[4] But this passage concludes with an acknowledgment that this interpretation was not unopposed: "Such (is the story told) of that curtain. There are also (objections) against this reason for its rending." We now proceed to these objections.

In Hebrews 10:19–20 (cf. also 6:19–20; 9:3) the author metaphorically describes the death of Jesus in terms of "the new and living way which he opened for us through the curtain, that is, through his flesh." When Brandon associates this text of Hebrews with a Jewish-Christian milieu, he overlooks the Hellenistic form of Christianity that is actually found in that epistle, but points inadvertently to what may be a better view of Mark 15:38.[5]

In Romans 3:25, Paul writes of Christ, "whom God put forward as an expiation by his blood, to be received by faith." The proximity of this expression to the ideas of Mark 15:38 (the opening of access to the place of expiation) and Mark 15:39 (the faith confession by the Roman centurion) makes the exploration of the parallel worthwhile. The verb "put forward" in Romans 3:25 suggests access to that which has previously been cut off.[6] The noun "expiation" renders the Greek *hilasterion*, which is a famous battlefield for commentators. Nygren may have the simplest, yet most logical suggestion in pointing out that the word stood in the Septuagint for the "mercy seat" as the place of annual expiation inside the veil of the Holy of Holies.[7] This view is encouraged by the fact that -*tērion* is a place ending, specifying *hilastērion* as "place of expiation."

Bultmann effectively argues that "Romans 3:24–25 leans on tradition which perhaps can be traced back to the earliest church," though he ascribes the phrase, "to be received by faith," to Paul himself.[8] His reasons for this are 1) reference to Christ as *hilastērion* occurs nowhere else in Pauline literature; 2) except where using traditional material (1 Cor. 10:16; 11:25, 27) Paul elsewhere speaks of the blood of Christ only in Romans 5:9; and 3) the idea of divine righteousness demanding expiation is alien to Paul. If correct, this argument would place the metaphor of the mercy seat put forward to public access not merely at the date of Paul's letter to the Romans (about A.D. 56), but at a time anterior to that, the time of the earliest church, the church that handed down to Paul the faith which he passes along in 1 Corinthians 15:3.

George Howard has undertaken to explicate "Romans 3:21–31 and the Inclusion of the Gentile World."[9] According to

Howard, confusion over the theology of Romans 3:21–31 (which is actually the whole of the epistle in nuce) arises from preoccupation with the faith-works problem always associated with Paul's theology. Howard holds that another theme, the universalism by which the Kingdom of God is now opened to the Gentiles, is the theme within which 3:21–31 is to be comprehended. This theme emerges in Romans 1:5, is reiterated in 1:16, and again in 2:10–11. The faith of Abraham in Romans 4 is the prototype of the "faith of Jesus" in 3:26, a faith specifically marked by blessedness upon all nations. Even if one quarrels with Howard over the dominance or the subdominance of the faith-justification motif, he cannot, in the light of Galatians 2:11–14, question that "faith" for Paul meant Gentile inclusion or it meant nothing.

Commentators vacillate over the question of whether Mark 15:38 reflects a symbolism of divine judgment upon Israel's unbelief or a symbolism of atonement now universally accessible to those who have faith (like the centurion). It is agreed by most that Paul's letter is written to the Romans (Rom. 1:7). If we concede to Brandon that Mark was addressed to Romans, is it not evident that Paul's letter (viz., Rom. 3:24–25) *would already have provided the context within which Mark 15:38–39 should be understood by the people in Rome*?

Two further considerations may be added to this. R. H. Lightfoot defends the atonement signification of Mark 15:38, pointing out that Mark uses "split" (*schizein*) only two times: once at the baptism (1:10) and once at the crucifixion (15:38).[10] The sacramental associations of the two passages cannot be denied, and Mark 15:38–39, in line with the Eucharist, may well provide a kind of haggadah upon the cross, the confession of the centurion constituting also a universalising *inclusio* that takes up again the idea of Mark 1:1 (". . . gospel of Jesus Christ, the Son of God").

In Matthew 27:51, the rending of the curtain lies in the same sequence of the passion narrative as it does in Mark. But Matthew adds to the account miraculous prodigies of redemption (27:51b–

53), an earthquake, and the emergence of dead saints from the tombs. This bears out what we suggest as Mark's idea. But the case with Luke is quite otherwise. Because Luke does not express a theology of atonement but depicts the passion along lines of a martyrdom,[11] the episode of the veil (Luke 23:45) takes place, contrary to Mark, before the outcry on the cross, which Luke has also altered.[12] Luke's description of the darkness that descends over the whole earth (23:44) sets a scene of darksome judgment for the splitting of the veil. The centurion's comment in Luke ("Certainly this man was innocent!") is not a baptismal confession as in Mark, but a protest against injustice. If, therefore, it were asserted of Luke's narration of the rending of the curtain that it expressed judgment rather than redemption, the argument would have to be conceded because both in the third Gospel and in Acts, Luke does show a pro-Roman tendency. Thus Marcion in the second century can assuredly lay hold of Luke (not Mark) for anti-Semitic purposes.

Thus Mark 15:38–39 can be understood along the lines of Romans 3:24–25 as a piece of pre-Pauline atonement thought already familiar to the Roman church, supposed recipients of the Markan Gospel. There is in Mark, as in all the prophets, judgment upon an impenitent Judaism, but this is not anti-Semitic, nor, for reasons shown, does Mark 15:38 belong to this category. Unless, therefore, one were compelled on some other grounds to find an allusion to the Flavian triumph in this passage, it could not, on its own merit, make such a suggestion.

Mark and Rome

The association of Mark with Rome has behind it early testimony of the church.[13] Numerous scholars (following a second-century Papias tradition recorded in Eusebius) connect

Mark with Peter's preaching and Peter with Rome. Other arguments for Rome are Mark's use of Latin loan words, the translation of Aramaic expressions, the explanation of Jewish customs, and Mark's major use by Matthew and Luke (which, in view of Mark's unpretentious literary claims, must have required the backing of a prominent church such as that in Rome). These and other arguments were carefully expounded by B. W. Bacon and many other scholars. Yet these premises have not gone uncontested. The historicity of the Papias logion connecting Mark and Peter has been seriously challenged.[14] The internal arguments (Latin loan words, etc.) could apply to many other Gentile church communities than that found in Rome, and C. F. Evans warns: "there is no sign of any knowledge of this Gospel in our earliest Christian document from Rome, the First Epistle of Clement, generally dated c. A.D. 96."[15]

At the present state of historical inquiry, a final solution to this problem cannot be given. That should, however, encourage our awareness of arguments offered against Mark's Roman origin.

Ernst Lohmeyer developed the view that Mark was a Galilean Gospel, because, among other reasons, it centers the ministry of Jesus and the calling of the apostles in Galilee, sustains a peculiar Galilean interest (e.g., Mark 14:70), even in the passion narrative, and promises toward the end a Galilean reunion (Mark 14:28; 16:7).[16] Willi Marxsen follows Lohmeyer and continues to find in Mark a preoccupation with Galilee, indicating on the basis of other evidence from Mark 13 that this Gospel was composed in Galilee between A.D. 67 and 68 after rumblings of Vespasian's impending conquest of the area were in the air.[17] L. E. Elliott-Binns and R. H. Lightfoot also supported Lohmeyer's preference for Galilee.[18]

This issue may be related to Mark's political apology in the following way. First, the Galilean origin of Mark, if eventually vindicated, would show that *within Palestine itself* existed political, cultural, or ethnic cleavages that issued in an abundance of abrasive and polemical exchanges, without appeal to Rome as a cause of them. "Galilee of the Gentiles" (Isa. 9:1; cf. Matt. 4:15) was already, before New Testament times, a bridgehead to the Gentile world. This is historically explainable from its subjugation and interpenetration by the Assyrians under Tiglath-pileser III in 738 B.C. (2 Kings 15:29). There is no rivalry like that between estranged kinsmen, as fully illustrated by Josephus' accounts of Zealot infighting during the Jewish war. Second, Marxsen and others in the Lohmeyer school should at least keep us aware that Mark's traditions have sources temporally antecedent to any final date or place of composition for the Gospel. Since it is Jesus' political inclinations that are ultimately at stake, rather than Mark's representation of them, historical method requires us to look beyond the present form of the Gospels (3) to the traditions they employed (2) before we have any index into the history of Jesus (1). The weight of this will be further evident in the discussions that follow.

The Tribute Question
Mark 12:13–17 (= Matt. 22:15–22 = Luke 20:20–26)

Pompey had taken Jerusalem in 63 B.C., and the Roman hegemony over Palestine continued throughout the New Testament period. That Jewish revolts were attempted in A.D. 6, 66, and 132—to mention only the more conspicuous ones—evidences the persistent fervor of Jewish nationalism and the smoldering resentment of Roman rule. It is this political context that gives the tribute question its cutting edge. Does Caesar have tax rights over Jews?

When the Roman tax census was imposed by Quirinius in A.D. 6,[19] Judas the Galilean called the people to resistance, "upbraiding them as cowards for consenting to pay tribute to Rome and tolerating mortal masters after having God for their Lord."[20] Throughout the life of Jesus the prospect of revolution lay close at hand. "Render to Caesar the things that are Caesar's, and to God the things that are God's" (Mark 12:17) apparently reflects, therefore, an accommodation to Roman imperialism, and this text, as it has come down through the tradition, would have been understood from the Zealot standpoint as a counsel of surrender. Verse 17, as Haenchen puts it in a classic understatement, "does not comply with the Zealot demand."[21]

The meaning that verse 17 has in Mark, must then, according to Brandon, be a reversal of the original meaning. "Jesus' pronouncement, therefore, was wholly in line with Zealot teaching, and so it must have been understood by those to whom it was originally addressed."[22] Eisler names the discoverer of this "true meaning of Jesus' saying about the tribute money" as none less than Richard Wagner, as set forth in his unfinished passion play, *Jesus of Nazareth*, composed before the revolution of 1848. Eisler comments:

"Render unto Caesar the things that are Caesar's" really means: "Throw Caesar's, i.e., Satan's, money down his throat, so that you may then be free to devote yourself wholly to the service of God." . . . Far from sanctioning the payment of tribute to Caesar, Jesus is wholly on the side of Judas of Galilee.[23]

Morris also evidences the Wagnerian flair:

It is as though the members of the Underground in Occupied Europe had asked a patriot whose judgment they respected whether they ought to help the Nazis ransack their country of its treasures, and had received the reply, "Give the Nazis what is coming to them!"[24]

Has Mark, as these statements imply, put upon the words of Jesus a sense diametrically opposed to their original intent? In the comments that follow, we intend to demonstrate that the implication ascribed in the Eislerian view to the political apology of the evangelist precedes the evangelist's time and, therefore, could not have been invented by him.

Mark 12:13–17 is a conflict paradigm in which the early church adduces Jesus' authoritative word as proof of a position or a solution to a problem. On controversy dialogues as a general category, Butlmann gives them a definite locus "in the apologetic and polemic of the Palestinian Church."[25] On the specific pronouncement story of Mark 12:13–17, he further states: "Only in v. 13 can we discern any of Mark's editorial work. There is no reason, in my view, for supposing that this is a community product."[26] This is a conservative statement, which implies that the church did not originate the paradigm out of its own needs but inherited it in the earliest Jesus traditions. Brandon is, consequently, on sound methodological ground when he acknowledges that Bultmann is "probably right in regarding verses 14–17 as a well-established piece of Christian tradition of pre-Markan origin," especially if he implies pre-Markan *Palestinian* origin.[27] To summarize, on form critical grounds the apparent accommodation to Rome or acknowledgement of Rome's right that is implied in Mark belongs already to the history of the Palestinian church and cannot, thus, be a Markan invention.

Rabbinical precedents corroborate this view. C. G. Montefiore saw no reason why a rabbi could not have given the reply of Mark 12:17: "It is certainly one which would not have been given by a Zealot. But the majority of the Rabbis were opposed to the Zealots. Most of them were not by any means anxious to revolt against Rome. . . ."[28] This position is expanded in the work of Israel Abrahams.[29] He cites the teachings of Rabbi Johanan ben Zakkai and his pupil Hananiah—both contemporaries of the revolt of A.D. 66—who counseled compliance with the tax requirements. Abrahams quotes a saying of R. Johanan in which tax evasion is denounced "as equivalent even to murder, idolatry, incest, and profanation of the Sabbath."[30]

Johanan b. Zakkai was the most famous rabbi of the period

of the war against Rome, A.D. 66–70. A famous saying ascribed
to him was: "O Galilee, Galilee, thou hatest the Torah; hence
wilt thou fall into the hands of robbers!"[31] Though variously
interpreted, the statement fixes in one way or another upon the
Roman occupation of Galilee early in the war.[32] Another famous
saying of Johanan predicts (on the basis of Zech. 11:1) the
destruction of the temple.[33] Brandon refers to the escape of
Johanan in a coffin during the siege of Jerusalem, but his remarks
do not make it clear that the leading religious figure of Judaism
counseled peace and refused to be a part of the fanatical Zealot
violence that was leading the city to ruin.[34] Ironically, Johanan
survived the war and afterward founded at Jamnia the continuing center for Palestinian Judaism.[35]

If, then, during the heightened passion of the period of the
war itself, figures like Johanan stand out against the course of
events dictated by Zealot ascendancy, it is quite arbitrary, to say
the least, to deny the existence of such beliefs in the decades
preceding the consummation of Zealot power. It becomes apparent again that there is no reason to ascribe to Mark a tendentious and revisionist role in the handling of this paradigm.
Such a view arises not from the text itself, but from presumptions
read into the text out of other considerations.

It is appropriate to insert at this juncture a comment on the
ethical import of the tribute paradigm in order to link up the
discussion with our theme, Jesus and the politics of violence.

It can scarcely be denied that Christian history, on the basis
of Mark 12:17 par. and its counterpart, Romans 13:1–7, has
evidenced a tendency to political passivity and the condoning of
institutional violence. Brandon's emphases may, therefore, have
a beneficial end if they help to restore the bipolar character of
political thought in the church and remove the sterile legalism that
has made so heavy a mark.

The philosophical issue underlying the right of revolution is
expressed in biblical thought under the rubrics of things of

Caesar/things of God, or, in the Pauline language, law/grace. That is, law is overthrown when it is no longer expressive of grace, no longer a vehicle of redemption. This is what Barth refers to in his commentary on Romans when he likens the law to a dry canal, i.e., one no longer carrying water and life.

In the categories of this book, revolution is legitimated or made necessary when law (or government) becomes the instrument of institutional violence. But revolution cannot have chronic existence, all of the boasts to the contrary notwithstanding. What is sought in revolution is another law in which the people are not exploited, abused, or tyrannized. The monotony of history is the vicious circle in which the overthrow of law is followed by another law that proves equally abusive. This problem is profoundly understood in the logion on tribute in that law is recognized as valid but with the limitation that it not be an agent of institutional violence.

This has been intelligently discerned in a comment by Ernst Käsemann on Romans 13 and the right of revolution:

. . . such a possibility could only exist when the possessors of political power are threatening and destroying in a radical way those ties which hold together a political community as a whole in bonds of mutual service. . . . [W]hen every concrete act of service within the individual's province takes on the character of participation in a common self-destruction—and in my view this possibility became reality for every man with eyes to see in the Third Reich (at least after Stalingrad)—then it also becomes impossible to deny to the Christian his right as a citizen to take part in revolution.[36]

It may seem paradoxical that Käsemann on the page preceding this quotation has said: "It is equally clear that there cannot be a Christian revolution as such." That paradox returns us to the dilemma of "Christians for violence."

Writers in the western tradition seldom devote serious attention to the possibility of nonviolent revolution.[37] The consequence, however, of closing out this option is that God's things continue to be rendered unto Caesar. Thus, for example, tax refusal, though it is not consistent with the right that government normally exercises, would not, in certain situations, be an impermissable tactic within Christian ethics. Obviously, many other forms of nonviolent civil disobedience are effective expressions of the Christian moral view, particularly when legal remedies have been found unavailing. The present disfavor of Christianity with movements of social change derives from the wooden way in which a middle-class, bureaucratic church leadership has lost the dialectical character of Mark 12:17 and surrendered to legalisms that encourage revolution. This revolution operates not only outside the church, but against the church, and, unfortunately, against the religion it claims to represent.

Simon the Zealot
Mark 3:18 (= Matt. 10:4 = Luke 6:15 = Acts 1:13)

"Cananaean," the name applied to the disciple Simon in Mark 3:18, is the Aramaic term for Zealot. Brandon urges that since Mark usually explains Aramaic expressions in his Gospel, his failure to do so in this case is due to his desire to conceal the political affiliation of Simon, an affiliation that was not merely part of his past, but continued during his apostleship.[38] If Simon had repudiated Zealotism, then Mark would not have retained this unbecoming appellative. Brandon asserts: "To use a modern parallel, it would have been tantamount to a convert's being still called 'the communist' by his co-religionists after leaving Communism for the Roman Catholic Church."[39]

The illustration is not a fortunate one. Whatever may be the official view on communism in the Catholic Church, it is already clear that among the rank and file in various places in the world, Christian and Communist are not mutually exclusive

terms. Millions of Christians now live under Communist governments and, generally speaking, in line with Mark 12:17 and
Romans 13, they do not seek to subvert these governments, but
may indeed find frequent occasion for positive support of them.[40]
Illustrations are not lacking in the west. Joe Wallace, author of
several books of poetry, is known as "Canada's labor poet." In
an interview on the Canadian Broadcasting Company on January
30, 1971, Wallace affirmed, "I am a good Catholic because I
am a good Communist, a good Communist because I am a good
Catholic."[41] From a devout Catholic family, he has seven brothers
who are priests. "I've had a difficult time reconciling Catholicism
with my Communism for others," he related in 1960, "but never
for myself."[42] On the Protestant side, Hewlett Johnson, dean of
Canterbury, was named "the Red Dean" by a Tory newspaper in
1940 after he had published the pro-Soviet book, *The Socialist
Sixth of the World*. The name stuck, though Johnson was never a
member of the Communist party. At the time of Johnson's death,
The New York Times reported that he was known as "a Communist, a crank, and a saint," having once said in a sermon. "if
Jesus were alive today, he would have been a Communist."[43] His
last sermon at Canterbury was on the power of nonviolence.

There are reasons within the New Testament period itself,
however, that should cause us caution in dealing with Simon the
Zealot. It is entirely possible that the term "Zealot" is inaccurately
used. Morton Smith recently canvassed all the references in
Josephus in "Zealots and Sicarii, Their Origins and Relation."[44]
Smith finds that there are serious reasons to defend the earlier
position of Kirsopp Lake that the Zealot party did not, as a party,
come into existence until the winter of 67–68, and is to be distinguished consequently from the followers of Judas the Galilean
whom Josephus calls Sicarii (*War*, 7: 253–54).[45] Smith defends
Thackeray's translation of *War* (2: 444) where Thackeray refers
to the followers of Menahem (a rebel leader) as "his . . . armed
fanatics." The designation "fanatics" renders the same Greek

word (*zēlotēs*) that modifies "Simon" in Mark 3:18. When Paul refers to himself as having been extremely *zealous* (*zēlotēs*) for the traditions of his fathers in Galatians 1:14, he employs this same word, but obviously in a sense that has not led commentators to say Paul was a member of the Zealot party. Günther Baumbach has also upheld Lake's careful distinction between Sicarii and Zealots, drawing on the Josephus references to show that the latter were a priestly resistance originating in Jerusalem during the war, while the Sicarii were Galilean-based, agrarian, more extreme types of revolutionaries.[46] The views of these writers oppose the interpretations of both Brandon and Hengel. Lake suggests the translation "Simon the zealous," for Mark 3:18, indicating the inadvisability of reading into the period of Jesus political developments that matured only in 66–70.[47] Thus when the King James Version rendered Luke 6:5 and Acts 1:13 with the proper name "Simon Zelotes" or "Simon called Zelotes," it is likely to have been a translation governed by a commendable, even if accidental, historical prudence.

The etymology of names is an insecure instrument for deriving historical information. This is clear from the fact that "Christ" in Christian usage gradually lost any concrete connections with its confessional origins that affirmed Jesus as the messiah, the anointed, and was understood as part of the name Jesus. Paul Winter may be correct in saying that by the time the Gospels were written, the evangelists no longer knew the names of the twelve.[48] The various lists of the apostles, though in general accord, cannot be fully harmonized no matter what textual variants are pursued. Yet the interest in the name Cananaean fosters the most fanciful notions. Constantin Daniel has suggested that the reed (Aramaic *qana*) given to Jesus as a derisive symbol of authority in Matthew 27:29—a suggestion taken up by Brandon[49]— is a veiled reference to Jesus' complicity with Zealotism, because *qana* sounds like *qannāyā*, Aramaic for Zealot![50] The "reed" (Greek *kalamos*) in Matthew 27:29 is apparently borrowed from

Mark 15:19 (=Matt. 27:30) and may well be an editorial (Matthaean) elaboration of the scene. When, therefore, Brandon and Daniel go from Greek *kalamos* back to Aramaic *qana* in order to get Zealotism into the passion narrative, it is as logical as saying that people named Cohen must be priests, because Hebrew *kōhēn* means "priest."[51]

The question of Simon the Zealot does point in the direction of a serious theological consideration in respect to the apostolic college and the ministry of Jesus. This was brought out as follows in Hengel's response to Brandon's comments on Simon:

The fact that one of the twelve bore the epithet "the Zealot" is repeated to the point of weariness and over-interpreted in its material content, but the fact that Jesus also called into his discipleship some of the taxgatherers, so hated by all nationally thinking Jews, and even cultivated close fellowship with them, is passed over. The positive attitude of Jesus towards the no less hated Samaritans is equally passed over in silence. The parable Luke x. 30–5 must have represented an affront not only to the Temple hierarchy but to every "patriotic" Jew, and that includes the Zealots in particular. Something similar is true of the saying Matt. viii. 11f = Luke xiii. 28f, which comes from the source Q. The question of the relationship of Jesus to the Torah (Mark vii. 15; ii. 27; x. 5ff; Matt. v. 21ff, 27ff, 33ff) which is quite fundamental to our estimate of Jesus, is also completely passed over.[52]

Jesus is the friend of publicans and sinners (Mark 2:13–17 par.), Bornkamm, whose methodology is consonant with modern critical standards, gives this feature of the Gospel tradition serious claim to historical validity.[53] In the same vein, W. R. Farmer made the outreach to publicans and sinners the core of "An Historical Essay on the Humanity of Jesus Christ."[54] Whatever may be true of the politics of Simon—we have adduced evidence against reading too much into it—it offers no clue whatever to the politics of Jesus. As well might we construe from Matthew the publican in Matthew 10:3 that Jesus was a champion of quisling politics, since that is the light in which publicans were regarded by their compatriots.

Implicit in the question that Brandon raises about the nationalism of Jesus is the factor of transcendence associated with Jesus in the christology of the New Testament. It must be made clear that the nationality of Jesus is not under dispute: Jesus was a Jew. When Mark 7:27 ("Let the children first be fed, for it is not right to take the children's bread and throw it to the dogs") is recorded in the tradition as a saying of Jesus to a Gentile woman, we should be reminded, as Brandon and others have done, of Jesus' nationality. The importance of nationality has been emphasized by Erik Erikson, while at the same moment he points to that which transcends it in human identity:

For membership in a nation, in a class, or in a caste is one of those elements of an individual's identity which at the very minimum comprise *what one is never not*, as does membership in one of the two sexes or in a given race. What one is never not establishes the life space within which one may hope to become uniquely and affirmatively what one is —and then to transcend that uniqueness by way of a more inclusive humanity. Thus was Jesus a Jew.[55]

Nor can we doubt in the history of christology that the Jewishness of Jesus gave ground as the Palestinian origins of the tradition yielded before the ecumenical spread of Christianity. The story of the Syrophoenician woman (Mark 7:24–30 par.), for example, is obviously told, even while acknowledging *what Jesus is never not*, to point beyond to the more inclusive humanity of which the Syrophoenician woman was the immediate provocation. Christianity and Judaism have this in common. It has been and should continue to be the basis on which they perform a mutual ministry to human need. To force Jesus, however, into the mold of a violent nationalism would not only falsify one of the essential elements of the humanity of Jesus, but also misrepresent the kind of humanity that Judaism itself has espoused. Zealotism, no matter what religious claims it made for itself, was, at best, heretical Judaism.

The Cleansing of the Temple
Mark 11:15–17 (=Matt. 21:12–13=Luke 19:45–46= John 2:13–17)

This paradigm occupies a pivotal position in determining what is alleged to be Mark's political apology. It will be recalled from the previous chapter how Eisler linked the episode with the insurrection passage from the Slavonic Josephus. Brandon's emphases are the following.

Jesus entered Jerusalem, then "looked round at everything" (Mark 11:11). Brandon asked whether this could have been "an act of reconnoitering" for the action of the coming day.[56] In any event, the attack on the temple was an anticipation of what the Zealots achieved in A.D. 66 when they finally seized the temple stronghold and held it against both Romans and non-Zealot Jews.[57] Jesus' action was "attended by violence and pillage."[58] The failure of the temple police to intervene in so rash an assault is due either to Mark having edited such police action out of the earlier description of it or to the fact that Jesus' collaborators were so numerous that temple police decided against intervention, awaiting a better occasion to sieze Jesus.[59] Mark creates the ecumenism of 11:17 ("house of prayer for all the nations") from Isaiah 56:7 for Roman consumption as part of his political apology.[60] The latter part of verse 17 ("But you have made it a den of robbers") from Jeremiah 7:11 is, in Mark's setting, double-pronged. On the one hand, to Mark's Roman audience "den of robbers" (i.e., brigands, insurrectionists) would refer to the Zealots holding the temple until finally crushed by the Romans in A.D. 70.[61] On the other hand, Mark lets the accusation fall from Jesus' lips upon the priestly aristocracy who are profaning the temple by cooperating with the Roman overlords.[62] Since

John 2:19 connects the temple cleansing with the saying, "Destroy this temple and in three days I will raise it up"—a saying that emerged later in connection with the trial before the Sanhedrin (Mark 14:58)[63]—it is likely that the utterance had something to do with the attack on the Temple banking establishment, money-changers, etc.[64] The charge that Jesus predicted the temple destruction is adroitly handled by Mark at 13:2 where the impersonal construction is employed ("There will not be left here one stone upon another, that will not be thrown down") to avoid the implication that Jesus himself is to be the agent of such destruction.[65] Jewish Christians in the pre-Markan period, who still clung to the temple cultus, must have been embarrassed by the negative attitude toward the temple on the part of Jesus. This explains why the prediction by Jesus of the temple destruction is presented (inconsistently with Mark 13:2) as a false accusation.

In this reconstruction Brandon assumes what may be called a typically "historical" viewpoint. That is, he wishes to cut through the tangle of apologetical overgrowth and expose what "really happened." Whether the various difficulties of Mark 11:15-19 will ever be satisfactorily resolved cannot be predicted, but it can be shown that Brandon's solution is unsatisfactory on the supposed historical grounds he proposes.

The problem can be laid out in a pair of alternative propositions:

1. If Jesus did plot the temple destruction and engaged in violence and pillage against it, it is not consistent with the sanctity in which Jewish Christianity held the temple prior to the writing of Mark.

2. If Jesus did not plot the temple destruction or engage in action aimed at its overthrow, then the charge laid against him in Mark 14:58 was false, as Mark 14:57-59 and John 2:21 state or imply.

Brandon rejects the first of these alternatives because he

wants to demonstrate throughout that Jesus was a Jewish nation-
alist with whom Jewish Christianity sustained direct ideological
continuity until A.D. 70. Passages such as Luke 2:49, 24:53, and
Acts 2:46 make it difficult to maintain that Jesus or Jewish
Christians could have looked upon the temple as expendable.[66]
Brandon must, then, assert on the one hand: "in view of the at-
tachment of the original community of Jesus' disciples to the
Temple, it is unlikely that Jesus, who himself frequented the
Temple, declared that he would destroy it."[67]

The second possibility (that Jesus was not, in fact, guilty
of the charge in Mark 14:58) is equally unacceptable to Brandon,
because this would lend historical credibility to Mark's account
of the trial of Jesus. So Brandon must, with discernible ambiguity,
state: "That the accusation should have been made at all, and
indeed, as it seems, constituted the chief charge against Jesus,
suggests that it could not have been completely groundless."[68]

Brandon's argument by no means resolves the conflict between the two propositions.

This discussion illustrates the impropriety of addressing
historical questions to the literature of the Gospels when its
theological intentions are not kept in the foreground of attention.
In a statement which sets intelligent limits to the "historical line
of questioning," Conzelmann has spoken of the episodes narrated
in Mark 11:

The complex of the entry into Jerusalem and the appearance of Jesus in
the temple offers an example of the unfruitfulness of the historical line
of questioning. Of course Jesus came sometime and somehow to Jerusalem. And of course at sometime he visited the temple. But with this
our sure knowledge is exhausted. All else remains supposition; why he
went to Jerusalem, how he appeared there, how long he could stay there
until he was arrested, etc. The contemporary preaching of these texts
cannot build on these conjectures, but, rather can only tie into the interpretation of the community which discovered this interpretation after
Easter.[69]

Brandon indicates an awareness of the historical complexities involved when he says of the evangelists' accounts of the temple cleansing, "It takes very little reflection, however, to realize that such a depiction can scarcely approximate to the truth."[70] One hopes that the definition of truth goes beyond the criterion of objective factuality, but that criterion alone should suffice to counter the effort to read into the record of Mark as "real history" something comparable to a Zealotic insurrection.

The following observations on the various accounts of the temple cleansing show how clearly the narrative is dominated by theological, as distinguished from historical, motifs and, further, indicate that historical conclusions other than those in the Eislerian tradition are defensible.

1. An important feature of Mark 11:17 is that the phrase "for all the nations" (from Isa. 56:7) is not found in any of the three parallels. Matthew 21:13 and Luke 19:46 clearly depend upon Mark 11:17, so one seeks for an explanation of the omission of the phrase, particularly when it is recognized, as most interpreters do, that as time progressed christology assumed a more transethnical character. Luke, in particular, would have seemingly relished the thought of "for all the nations." What we probably encounter here is the familiar tendency of the two subsequent evangelists to reduce the size of the Markan narration. Thus Mark requires 65 words to tell the story, Matthew, 45, and Luke, 25.[71]

Following the "historical line of questioning," T. W. Manson produced a persuasive interpretation of this pericope, arriving at conclusions opposite to those of Brandon.[72] According to this view, Jesus cleanses the court of the Gentiles.[73] Josephus described the barrier and warning inscription in Greek and Latin that forbade access by non-Jews to the inner perimeters of the Temple that lay within the outer court of the Gentiles.[74] Thus the profanation of the court of the Gentiles by the merchants and moneychangers prohibited to Gentiles that measure of access to

God's presence that was already provided in the Mosaic system for "the nations." Jesus' decisive action, in turn, signaled the restoration of the proper use of the court of the Gentiles as a place of prayer for all nations and, in the eye of the evangelist, signaled Jesus' messianic ecumenism.[75] This interpretation has to its advantage that the crucial phrase, "for all the nations," derives from the book of Isaiah. Mark is assuredly impressed with the ecumenicity of the story, but that element cannot have originated in A.D. 70 or 71 any more than it could be claimed that the outreach of Jesus had no antecedents in Isaiah or Jonah or in numerous other prophetic books.

It is probably in this context that the meaning of the cursing of the fig tree (Mark 11:12–14, 20–25) is to be comprehended. Mark has "sandwiched" the temple cleansing into the fig tree episode, suggesting that the judgment it figuratively pronounces is related to the ethnic exclusiveness polemicized in Mark 11: 15–19.

The irony, and yet the substantiation, of this exposition is that modern Christianity stands in the very position of Judaism in the first century. That is, despite all the ecumenical features that belong to the basis of Christianity in the New Testament, it has so frequently been joined to white supremacist practices and institutional racism that the rise of the nonwhite people inevitably condemns Christianity as the "white man's religion." In this way it is not only Judaism, but also Christianity, that succumbs to Zealotism.

2. Brandon is probably correct when he emphasizes that the later evangelists expanded Mark's portrayal of the pacific Christ, even if it cannot be granted that Mark's record represents an initial historical distortion. This factor may be at play in the Johannine account of the temple cleansing. John 2:13–22 also further demonstrates how theological interests dominate the tradition, interests not appreciably different from Mark's despite its earlier composition.

John 2:15 is correctly translated in the British Revised

Version, "He . . . cast all out of the temple, both the sheep and the oxen." As Hoskyns and Davey emphasize: "not all the merchants . . . but all the animals."[76] The correct translation is also found in the American Standard Version, Weymouth, Goodspeed, Alford's Greek Testament, and the Good News Translation (1966), which reads, "He . . . drove all the animals out of the Temple, both the sheep and the cattle." This means that the King James Version, the Revised Standard Version, the New English Bible, the Moffatt Bible, the Jerusalem Bible—to specify some of the major translations—do not convey the correct idea.

Bultmann refers to the clause in question ("both the sheep and the cattle") as a case of "clumsy [schlechte] apposition," being an editorial addition. He points out that the correlative conjunction, "both . . . and" (te . . . kai), is not elsewhere attested in John or in the Epistles of John.[77] It agrees with Bultmann's use of the term "clumsy" that verse 16 singles out the sellers of pigeons, while in verse 15 it is the animals rather than the sellers of them which are specified. Macgregor, following the historical line of questioning, comments: "But naturally it would be impossible to 'drive out' the birds in their cages, and therefore Jesus bids their owners 'Away with these!' "[78] It should be observed that the Markan version knows nothing of the whip (John 2:15) nor the appositional clause on the sheep and cattle.

Bultmann is probably correct in treating "both the sheep and the cattle" as an editorial insertion. The fourth evangelist did not work from the Markan text, but from a source related to the Markan tradition, in a way yet unexplained. The appositional clause can be traced to Psalm 8:6–7 (Hebrew, verses 7–8). This psalm is used messianically in Hebrews 2:6–8 and 1 Corinthians 15:27. It was useful to New Testament christology not only because it referred to the son of man (Ps. 8:4), but because it expressed the humiliation-exaltation motif exemplified in Philippians 2:6–11 and in the gnostic redeemer myth.[79] The appositional construction of "sheep and oxen" is also observed from the Psalm: "thou has put all things under his feet, all sheep and oxen, . . ."[80]

It is clear from this how John transcended historical interests, using the tradition as a vehicle for christological midrash.
John seemed to avoid the implication to be derived from Mark
that the force of the expulsion was directed against the persons
involved.

The customary portrayals of Jesus wielding something like
a cat-o'-nine-tails are falsely deduced from the Johannine account. Jesus is described in John 2:15 as "making a whip of
cords." That is, on the spot he fashioned something. The word for
"cords" (*skoinia*) means "reeds" or "rushes."[81] Presumably to
avoid the impression that this might have been a weapon of injury, before the Latin loan word for "whip," *fragellion*, is found
in the Bodmer Papyri (P[66, 75]) the qualifying particle *hōs*,
meaning "a kind of," or "something like." The correctness of this
reading is recognized by Raymond Brown in the Anchor Bible.[82]
In view of the pervasive christological interests of the narrative,
Westcott is probably correct in his comment that the "whip" in
John is a symbol of messianic authority.[83] Malachi 3:1–5 (the
purging messenger who suddenly comes to the temple) informs
and shapes the christology of this story in all four of the Gospels.[84] Other prooftexts (to summarize) that have shaped the
tradition are: Isaiah 56:7 and Jeremiah 7:11 (= Mark 11:17
par); Zechariah 14:21 (= Mark 11:16); Psalm 8:6–7 (= John
2:15); Psalm 69:9 (= John 2:21). Obviously, in all four of the
Gospel accounts, the evangelists did not write in order to supply
historical data but to present in a post-Easter fashion the messiahship of Jesus.

Summary and Conclusion

The ethical ideograms that have been drawn from the
cleansing of the temple in Christian history cannot be regarded
as anything less than a disaster. A passage in Ellul shows how
soon this began:

Apparently, the first to act on this idea [of righteous violence] were the anchorites of the Nile valley, those hairy, savage hermits of the third and fourth centuries, who periodically descended on the great cities of the valley (especially Alexandria) and, wielding their long gnarled sticks, set about beating up people and smashing everything in sight. As they saw it, theirs was a kind of purifying violence. In the face of corruption of morals rampant in Egypt at that time, they proclaimed the imminence of the stern judgment of God, and drove home their proclamation by their violent actions. They took upon themselves to punish sinners here and now and to manifest God's judgment on the world in concrete ways. Thus these terrible anchorites were motivated by a prophetic and spiritual concern. They took their cue from the celebrated biblical passage which tells how Jesus whipped the merchants [sic] and drove them from the temple.[85]

In the Bible of Christian nationalists, the "whip" of Jesus is rapidly escalated into the most sophisticated weapons of mass destruction and joined to the righteous wrath that inspires "holy war." If Brandon's reconstruction of the history of the temple cleansing were taken seriously, we could only anticipate the moral distortions that have already ravaged Mark 11:15–17 par. from the earliest period. To illustrate, one reviewer of Arnold Cone's *Black Theology and Black Power* commends Cone's defense of black hatred and his program of black liberation, but faults him for his timidity about violence:

The problem with revolutionary violence, according to Cone, rests with Jesus, who seems to be portrayed in the New Testament as being "against violence as a proper redress." Such a statement comes as a surprise: having challenged many traditional assumptions throughout his book, Cone does not challenge with equal vigor the authority of the New Testament text itself. Despite the fact that there is an increasing body of evidence which indicates that Jesus was probably violent and indeed a Zealot, Cone appears quite relaxed in accepting a stereotyped Jesus who glides through the Gospels doing good. Cone accepts this view of Jesus as history but rejects his current relevance for moral guidance. How unfortunate it is that Dr. Cone suggests that we do not need to ask today, "What would Jesus do?" On the contrary, if we accept the fact that God was in Christ, it would seem that the question, "What would Jesus do?" must have perennial relevance. Would not the question of violence be easy to deal with if we accept the fact that Jesus was then a Zealot and now, as Cone himself says, a black man?[86]

White racist violence, both personal and institutional, symbolized in the Ku Klux Klan, makes black violence understandable and, as many affirm, inevitable. (Nor should it be forgotten that most Klansmen consider themselves religious, churchgoing men.) If, however, the black community achieves its power on the same premises and by the same means that white power has been achieved, the monotony of human cruelty is not going to be relieved, and the language that applies "Christian" and "biblical" sanctions to this monotony will have to be cleansed from some quarter not now in sight.

This discussion has attempted to show how, on both exegetical and historical grounds, the "historical line of questioning" pursued in Mark's supposed political apology can be opposed. It is neither morally nor exegetically insensible to see in the temple cleansing a revolutionary action on the part of Jesus, if that is not distorted in the direction of Zealotism. In the fact of this paradigm alone, it cannot be intelligently maintained that Jesus passively accepted whatever wrong was perpetrated, even though some would caricature the nonviolence of Jesus by insisting that the non-resistance exemplified in Matthew 5:39 were the sum and total of Jesus' teaching and conduct.

In this chapter we have found no compelling evidence in the texts considered to demonstrate that Mark concealed or twisted the history of Jesus to curry favor with Rome by scapegoating Jerusalem. We have shown instances where the tradition recorded by Mark goes back to a time much earlier than the fall of Jerusalem. The conflicts mirrored in this tradition not only go back to the Palestinian church but also unveil struggles, judgments, and tensions within Judaism itself. If Jesus' attack on the corruption of the temple and its worship were to be construed in some way as anti-Semitic, then the prophets who did the same thing long before Jesus must also be judged as anti-Semitic. Likewise, the ecumenism ascribed to Jesus in the earliest traditions cannot be construed as prejudice against Jewry, unless one is prepared to deny that within Jewry, irrespective of the New Testament, the rudiments of such ecumenism are also to be found.

If, therefore, the postulation of a political apology in Mark related to the Flavian triumph of A.D. 71 lacks confirmatory evidence, it remains now to look at Mark on its own terms to discover within it the features by which we may discern the uniqueness of the evangelist's viewpoint and intention.

IV. MARK WITHOUT POLITICS

In the two previous chapters, the discussion has been largely controlled by an apologetical interest, namely, the critical examination of the Eisler-Brandon thesis regarding Jesus' complicity with political violence against Rome in first-century Palestine. At this point, our inquiry assumes a different character. Mark must be allowed to speak for itself. The total design and message of the book must be seen in panorama, so that the distinguishing lineaments of the writer's intention may be discovered.

For the sake of clarity, the argument of the chapter can be summarized as follows. William Wrede pioneered modern Markan studies by drawing attention to the Messianic Secret as Mark's "key." Why does Jesus command his messiahship to be kept secret? Wrede held that the Secret was Mark's device, a kind of dogmatic tour de force, for fusing a nonmessianic history of Jesus with the church's belief in him as Messiah. Following Wrede, it can be shown that the Secret motif does, indeed, belong to the connective material of the evangelist rather than to the nucleus of the inherited tradition. Further, it is seen that the whole structure of Mark is held together by the strange idea of a Messiah manifested yet hidden, the secret epiphany. Wrede's view on the messianic consciousness of Jesus can also be defended (against Schweitzer). Against Wrede, it is to be seen that the Secret is not a dogmatic invention, a hoax of orthodox belief, but a philosophy of revelation designed to correct a mistaken, triumphal notion of Messiah by pitting against it the theology of the cross. This corresponds to the christology imbedded in 1 Corinthians 2 and lends to Mark the character of a passion narrative with an extended introduction. Mark's theology of the cross is also a moral corrective in that the passion sets the tone for discipleship. This is further illustrated by observing its points of reference in prophetism, apocalypticism, and gnosticism. Thus Mark conveys a moral understanding that stands over against power, whether it is Rome's or Jerusalem's.

The Secret Messiah

William Wrede died in 1916 after teaching New Testament studies at Breslau for twenty years. He was strongly moved toward the application of historical criteria to biblical studies, believing that established doctrinal concepts (*Lehrbegriffe*) that predetermined the message of the New Testament had to be overruled to allow each portion of the literature to express its uniqueness.[1] He also resisted the concept of canonical versus non-canonical writings on the ground that this too was a wrongful subordination of historical to dogmatic values. His most influential publication was *Das Messiasgeheimnis in den Evangelien* (*The Messianic Secret in the Gospels*) in 1901.

The Messianic Secret in Mark has three facets: 1) Jesus' demand that the demons (1:34, 3:12), his associates (8:30, 9:9, 9:30), and those healed (1:44–45, 5:43, 7:36, 8:26) keep silent about his identity; 2) emphasis upon the disciples' lack of understanding (4:40–41, 6:52, 8:16–21, 9:10, 32), 3) the theory of parable as riddle (4:10–12).[2] Prior to Wrede Mark was understood to represent a gradual unfolding of the messianic identity of Jesus, a disclosure held back by Jesus' awareness of a need to educe from the disciples in progressive steps an awareness of his unique vocation as the Messiah who suffers redemptively in line with Isaiah 52:13–53:12. The decisive affirmation of Peter in Mark 8:29, "You are the Christ!," was the discovery of the Secret as Jesus' commendation of Peter (as expressed in Matthew 16:17) confirms.

Instead of these customary explanations built up from appropriate elements of Christian catechism and pieced together from a selection of texts drawn from all the Gospels, Wrede insisted that Mark must be examined on its own merits. For example, there is no commendation of Peter's confession in Mark such as that attested in Matthew, so it should not be read into Mark's understanding.[3] There is, moreover, no buildup in Mark toward the disclosures climaxing in the confession on the road to Caesarea Philippi (Mark 8:27–9:1), because in Mark 2:19–20 the passion is already predicted, while also in 4:11 it has already been asserted that the mystery of the kingdom has been disclosed to the disciples.[4] After the confession the disciples still do not understand, and even the first so called "successful" period of the ministry, according to Mark 3:6, already lies under the shadow of the cross. So Mark's "he began to teach them that the Son of man must suffer many things" (Mark 8:31) does not fit a chronological or psychological development any more than Matthew's use of the same idea.[5]

The Secret motif in Mark is, then, replete with contradictions: The public performing of miracles is not consistent with the injunction to be silent. It conflicts with open messianic sayings such as those in Mark 2:10; 28, and with the "triumphal" entry into Jerusalem.[6] The parable Secret (Mark 4:10–12) is not consistently executed, because the adversaries in Mark 12:12 comprehend full well the meaning of the Wicked Husbandmen.

Besides that, the injunctions to silence are not obeyed but openly violated (e.g., Mark 1:45, 7:24, 36), a violation that cannot be explained, according to Wrede, either by Jesus' inability to guarantee compliance or to Mark's sticking to the historical data.[7]

These difficulties make it clear that the Secret is not a historical fact, but serves to synthesize in Mark what was historically the nonmessianic career of Jesus with the church's belief in him as the Messiah on the basis of the resurrection.[8] This conclusion of Wrede serves to explain why Schweitzer designated his book as "thoroughgoing scepticism." Yet we hope to show presently that Wrede's position on the messianic consciousness of Jesus can be defended against Schweitzer's attack upon it, even though his explanation of the Secret must be subjected to considerable revision. Wrede's monumental importance was to focus attention upon the Messianic Secret as the hermeneutical key to Mark and to encourage the investigation of that Gospel on premises not controlled by theological dogma or the influence of the other evangelists. Wrede's concentration on the Secret motif is vindicated by the discovery that the Secret does not appear in the core of the traditional units of the material, but in the connective, i.e., editorial, material by which the units were placed in sequence.

The Secret as Editorial Device

Wrede's investigations of Mark stood on the threshold of the form critical movement, that program by which the separate units of the tradition were scrutinized in respect to the churchly situation giving to the individual pericope its unique function and form. K. L. Schmidt reinforced Wrede's assessment of the editorial origin of the Secret by assigning it to the editorial "framework" of the history.[9]

In the following table are listed all the texts related to Mark's concealment theme. In the left column (1) is the page number in Aland's *Synopsis* followed (2) by the page number in *Gospel Parallels*, edited by B. H. Throckmorton. The text reference is given in the right column. In each case where it seems clear that the Secret theme resides in the editorial framework, an asterisk (*) is placed before the reference. The references in Matthew and Luke are added after the references in Mark, where parallels exist. Since it belongs to the identification of Mark's uniqueness as a Gospel writer to observe what Matthew and Luke have done in the transmission or omission of his emphases, it is stated in parenthesis following each parallel reference whether the subsequent evangelists have omitted (om.) the Secret, retained (ret.) it, or modified (mod.) it. Where omission or modification occurs, it constitutes further evidence that the Secret in Mark represents an editorial rather than a traditional interest.

Page in Synopsis (1)	Page in Gospel Parallels (2)	Reference
55	18	*Mark 1:34 = Matt. 8:16 (om.) = Luke 4:41 (ret.)
59	32	*Mark 1:44–45 = Matt. 8:4 (mod.) = Luke 5:14–16 (mod.)
69	53	*Mark 3:12 = Matt. 12:16 (mod.) = Luke 6:19 (om.)
175–76	66	*Mark 4:10–12 = Matt. 13:10–15 (mod.) =Luke 8:9–10 (mod.)
186–87	72	*Mark 4:40–41=Matt. 8:26 (mod.)=Luke 8:25 (mod.)
192	75	*Mark 5:43 = Matt. 9:26 (om.) = Luke 8:56 (ret.)
211	81	*Mark 6:52 = Matt. 14:33 (om.)
222	85	*Mark 7:36 = Matt. 15:30 (om.)
227–28	87	*Mark 8:16–21 = Matt. 16:7–12 (mod.)
228	88	*Mark 8:26

231	89	*Mark 8:30 = Matt. 16:20 (ret.) = Luke 9:21 (ret.)
238	92	*Mark 9:9–10 = Matt. 17:9 (mod.) = Luke 9:36 (mod.)
243	94	*Mark 9:30 = Matt. 17:22 (om.) = Luke 9:43 (om.)
243	94	*Mark 9:32 = Matt. 17:23 (om.) = Luke 9:45 (ret.)

To summarize: Fourteen occurrences of the Secret idea in Mark produce a total of twenty-three parallels in the other two Gospels. In only five of these is Mark's idea carried over without modification. Four of these are in Luke, which may indicate Luke's penchant by comparison with Matthew to incorporate his source as it is. In eight instances the Secret is omitted (six times in Matthew; two in Luke), not to mention those five instances where no parallel exists. Despite the relativities that enter into the question of whether a parallel modifies or retains Mark's idea, it should be clear from this that the authors of Matthew and Luke did not feel any strong compulsion to carry over the Secret as presented in Mark's form. That could also attest to the editorial status of it.

Without engaging in an exhaustive treatment of all the Markan concealment texts, it will be useful at least to illustrate what is meant by the assertion (indicated by the asterisk) that the Secret comes in the editorial framework rather than the pre-edited core of the traditional material.

Mark 1:34, the first of the examples in the table above, gives a summary of Jesus' healing and exorcism, the "whole city" being gathered at evening about the door. Summaries are by nature editorial, since they go beyond the report of individual episodes and deal in total impressions. The time reference in verse 32, "that evening at sundown" (a Markan pleonasm pruned off by Matthew 8:16 and Luke 4:40), points back to the Sabbath named in Mark 1:21. The "Sabbath" in 1:21b along with "into the synagogue"—"immediately" (*euthus*) is patently a sign of Mark's editor—also comprises with 1:22 a generalization (cf. Matt. 7:28b–29) borrowing these temporal references from the paradigm in Mark 1:23–28.[10] "The whole city" in 1:33 is another Markan hyperbole like "all the country of Judea" and "all the people of Jerusalem" in Mark 1:5. Thus the entire section embraced in Mark 1:32–34 bears strong editorial fingerprints. Matthew 8:16 eliminates the Secret injunction in Mark 1:34b and adds in a characteristic Matthaean way a formulary quotation from Isaiah 53:4. Luke 4:41 retains Mark's idea, making explicit who Jesus is recognized to be: the Christ, reflecting probably Luke's interest in the messianic chrism specifically mentioned in Luke 4:18 and implicit in the preceding baptism and temptation accounts of Luke. Hence Mark 1:34b is editorial.

Mark 1:44–45 is the second example. Bultmann held that 44a ("and [he] said to him, 'See that you say nothing to anyone' ") is an editorial addition contradicting 44b ("but go, show yourself to the priest, and offer for your cleansing what Moses commanded, for a proof to the people").[11] H. J. Ebeling argued, however, that 44a is merely the negative side of the command to show himself to the priest and thus had nothing to do with the panoramic idea of secrecy.[12] This objection seems unsupportable on the premise that verse 45 bears out the epiphany aspect of the Secret—the healed man tells it everywhere—so that, just as in Mark 7:24 and 36, the command to silence only results in its being broken. Thus Mark 1:44–45 carries out Mark's unique philosophy that "there is nothing hid, except to be made manifest; nor is anything secret, except to come to light" (4:22). Matthew 8:4 abbreviates Mark, cutting off Mark 1:45 entirely, thus keeping the Secret but abandoning the epiphany. The contrast between "openly enter a town" (Mark 1:45a) and "out in the country" (1:45b) enforces the air of concealment, while the "and people came to him from every quarter" concludes on the epiphany theme again. Luke 5:16 adds to Jesus' retreat in Mark the purpose of prayer ("he withdrew to

the wilderness and prayed"). This is a characteristic Lukan alteration as evidenced in the change introduced by Luke 3:21 into
Mark 1:10, Luke 6:12 into Mark 3:13, or Luke 11:1 by comparison with Matthew 6:9. It also demonstrates how Luke nul-
lifies the manifestation motif found in Mark's final notice (Mark
1:45b) that people came to him from everywhere. So Mark 1:44–
45 is also editorial.

The third example in the table is Mark 3:12. The entire section, Mark 3:7–12, is an editorial generalization like that in
Mark 1:32–34. In 3:7–12, Mark portrays the cosmic confrontation between the superpowers. James Robinson has perceptibly
affirmed that exorcism confrontations in Mark not only contrast
the demoniac as agent of Satan versus Jesus as bearer of the
Holy Spirit, but: "there is a second contrast within the exorcism
stories: that between the violence and destructiveness of the
demon in the human he possesses, and the tranquillity and communion in the scenes of Jesus with the liberated person."[13]

Koester questions whether this contrast belongs to the peculiar Markan view of history as over against the general category
of exorcism or healing narratives common to the literature of that
time.[14] In so far as Mark frames the exorcism or healing stories
with the idea of the Messianic Secret, as in 3:12, it is Mark's own
viewpoint we meet, a point not contested by Koester. Robinson's
comment singles out the utopian-eschatological scenario established for and by the ministry of Jesus in a way we also encounter
in the Sermon on the Mount. Matthew's handling of Mark 3:12
is very interesting.[15] At Matthew 12:17 is introduced a Servant
prophecy from Isaiah 42:1–4 as a formulary quotation. Matthew
illustrates in this case how the Servant idea gains entry by way
of commentary upon earlier tradition, for "He will not wrangle or
cry aloud, nor will any one hear his voice in the streets" (Matt.
12:19) becomes Matthew's explanation of the Secret he derives
in Matthew 12:16 from Mark 3:12. Luke 6:17–19 uses the
Markan summary of the healing ministry as an introduction to

the Sermon on the Plain, but cuts off Mark 3:12, probably because of its inconsistency with the public character both of the healing and teaching ministry.

These examples suffice to show what we mean by declaring that the Messianic Secret in Mark is an editorial creation.[16] We have tried to show that Wrede's isolation of the Messianic Secret was of pioneering importance in discerning Mark's programmatic viewpoint and intention. Perhaps no phrase, therefore, has received wider coinage as a characterization of Mark than the one expressed by Martin Dibelius: "a book of secret epiphanies."[17] This can be reinforced by demonstrating that the entire structure of Mark is permeated by the Secret motif. We proceed to that in the following section, showing at the same time how the Secret and the Passion stand in close conjunction.

The Structure of Mark

Redaction criticism, or study of the evangelists' method of editing materials of the tradition, beneficially restores an awareness of the total unity of each of the Gospels. This does not, however, overcome the persistent influence of the unedited material, as we discern in the visibility, despite emendations, in Matthew and Luke of the Secret idea of Mark. Mark does not escape contradictions that attend his editorial program. Mark 2:10 and 28 thus break Mark's general rule to avoid messianic titles applied by Jesus to himself before his arrest, because the source here employed by Mark already utilized the Son of Man title.[18] Also, when Mark 4:36 takes up again the boat scene—having already appeared in Mark 4:1—the evangelist seems to gloss over the intervening material that leaves the boat scene behind. On this account, it should not be expected that anything approaching complete editorial coherence is to be found in Mark or in any of the Gospels. We propose, however, to explore the structure of Mark along two lines. First is the Secret theme already discussed. Second is the well-worn axiom from Martin Kähler that the Gospels are "passion narratives with extended introductions."[19] In the following material, we shall attempt to show that both of these themes (Secret and Passion) tie Mark together throughout and relate to one another intimately, though the one (Secret) is part of the redaction while the other (Passion) is integral to the earliest tradition. We begin with the Passion narrative, broadly defined to include Mark 11:1 through 16:8, because Mark's earlier material clearly points forward to, that is, introduces, the Passion.

Recent efforts by Eta Linnemann to establish Mark's authentic ending by appeal to Matthew 28:16–20 and the Koine text of Mark 16:15–20 were effectively countered by Kurt Aland.[20] The final limit of Mark must remain at 16:8, as effectively argued by R. H. Lightfoot, unless decisive new manuscript evidence is discovered.[21] Mark 16:8 is pervaded with the idea of *mysterium* and signals in a consummate gesture the evangelist's concept of revelation. After the Jerusalem entry and the temple cleansing of 11:1–18, one might be inclined to speak of the "long intervening passage which has been worked in by the evangelist" until his account of the Passion resumes in 14:1, but the allegory of the Wicked Husbandman as it now stands in 12:1–12 is a churchly reflection on the crucifixion.[22] David Daube has, furthermore, argued that the four questions of the "haggadha of the Seder" (the service on Passover eve) underlie the fourfold questioning of Mark 12:14, 23, 28, and 35, providing a reason why these paradigms were connected with the Jewish Christian Passover.[23] The conflict paradigms of Mark 12, as we shall presently see by comparison with earlier conflict narratives in 2:1–3:6, point toward the crucifixion while expressing early Palestinian confrontations of the church. Connections between the Passion and Mark 13 articulated by Lightfoot have recently been amplified by Charles Cousar.[24] It must be emphasized that *nowhere in Mark 11:1 through 16:8 is the special redactionary device of the Messianic Secret to be found.* Even if the manifestation command of 16:7 be ascribed (by contrast to the strange silence of 16:8) to the redactor, the passage lies outside the material wherein Jesus' relationship to Rome and Jerusalem climaxes and where, presumedly, Mark's political apology would make itself most heavily felt. The absence of Mark's major editorial theme attests the traditional as opposed to editorial character of the passion story.

The section 8:27–10:52 is a bridge toward the Passion, the way from Galilee to Jerusalem. It attests the Secret motif frequently (see previous table) and is integrated by the rejection of Peter's confession in 8:27–33. A Passion prediction in 8:31 is followed by a second in 9:31 and a third in 10:33–34. The predictions so clearly conform to the Passion that Mark is soon to narrate that the editorial, connective function of the whole section is apparent.[25] Older emphasis upon the Caesarea Philippi episode as Mark's "watershed" are quite correct as an identification of Mark's editorial program, but are incorrect as an index either to the objective or subjective history of Jesus. By its welding together of discipleship and Passion, this section sets forth the unique moral understanding that the Markan Gospel communicates, a point presently to engage us more fully.

Mark 6:7–8:26 derives its unity from the two parallel accounts of the feeding of the multitude. The details of the parallel have been charted and perceptively explained by Robert Grant as follows:[26]

Mark 6:33–7:37	*Mark 8:1–26*
five loaves, two fish (6:38)	seven loaves, a few fish (8:5–7)
twelve baskets full (6:43)	seven baskets full (8:9)
five thousand fed (6:44)	four thousand fed (8:9)
by boat to Bethsaida (6:45)	by boat to Dalmanutha (8:10)
controversy with Pharisees (7:1–23)	controversy with Pharisees (8:11–12)

question of children's bread (7:27–28)

exorcism of a demon (7:24–30)

through Sidon (7:31)

healing of a deafmute by material means (7:32–36)

injunction to secrecy (7:36)

allusion to Isa. 35:5–6 (7:37)

question of bread (8:16–17)

meaning of feedings (8:18–21)

to Bethsaida (8:22)

healing of a blind man by material means (8:22–25)

injunction to secrecy (8:26)

(no allusion to Isa. 35, but "blind" is in Isa. 35:5)

In 8:14–21 Mark grasps the opportunity to emphasize the obtuseness of the disciples in line with Isaiah 6:9–10 (Mark 8:17–18), which has placed its peculiar stamp on Mark 4:10–12 as the trademark of the teaching of Jesus. In Mark 7:37 there is a reflection on Isaiah 35:5–6, where, in the eschatological restoration, the blind and deaf, the lame and dumb receive healing. In Mark 7:32–36 occurs the messianic healing of the man deaf and speechless, while in 8:22–26 is narrated the recovery of the blind man's vision.[27] This leaves only one omission from the fourfold restoration of Isaiah 35:5–6, namely, the lame man who will "leap like a hart." This omission agrees with Mark's soteriology, related in his cryptic way to the secrecy/revelation paradox. That is, the cure of the lame man does not "fit" the categories of seeing and hearing, believing and confessing. Mark 6:7–13 is broken apart from its conclusion in verses 30–32 by the sandwiching in of the martydrom of John (6:14–29). Heinz-Dieter Knigge[28] ascribes this to an analogue carried out in Mark between the apostolic mission pursuant to the death of Jesus and the apostolic mission in this case (6:7–13, 30–32) associated with the death of John.[29]

Mark 3:7–6:6 is a unit wherein the subsection 4:1–20 forms a major index to Mark's interests and methods.[29] Jeremias has listed the reasons for taking Mark 4:14–20 as an allegorical, noneschatological commentary on the eschatological Parable of the Sower in verses 3–9.[30] The setting (verses 1–2) and the connective material in verses 10–13 are editorial.[31] Mark leaves his editorial signature in the predestinarian concealment motif of 4:12, reflecting upon Isaiah 6:9–10. The reference to insiders and outsiders in 4:11 is a traditional distinction as attested in 1 Corinthians 5:12–13 and 1 Thessalonians 4:12.[32] But Mark uses it in his own way. He emphasizes in 4:12 and 4:34 that the disciples receive special explanations (like 4:14–20), but the failure to reconcile this with the disciples' obtuseness (cf. 6:52 and 8:17–21) can be ascribed either to the imperfect execution of his program by the evangelist or his desire to emphasize the baffling, supernatural aspect of the Secret epiphany paradox.

Mark 2:1 through 3:6 is commonly assigned to a controversy section with a Passion prediction of another sort: "The Pharisees went out, and immediately held counsel with the Herodians against him, how to destroy him." The miraculous healings and astounding teaching of Jesus in this section are not, therefore, eulogies of the divine man in the customary Hellenistic sense, but they are overshadowed by the Passion of which the Markan redaction is consistently aware.

Mark 1 also closes with a series of aretalogies (sagas of the divine man) into which Mark's *Geheimnismotiv* has been woven at 1:34 and 1:44–45. Even the call of the disciples in 1:16–20 approaches a miracle story in character since the disciples' response —Mark's use of "immediately" (*euthus*) in verses 18 and 20 seems to be emphatic—has more of a metahistorical than a histrical tone to it. The command to silence in 1:25 parallels the rebuke of the sea in Mark 4:39 and belongs more to the mythological worldview than to the redactor's idea of secrecy. Marxsen has successfully demonstrated how the baptism, temptation, and inaugural preaching in Galilee (1:9–15) are built up in blocks from the memory of the crucifixion. "Arrested" in 1:14 points directly to the Passion of Jesus, showing again how Mark mirrors Jesus with John and vice versa.[33] On the basis of Jesus' contacts with the synagogue (e.g., Mark 1:21) and the priesthood as illustrated in 1:40–45, Keck has concluded: "One must also see that Mark makes clear that Jesus is not bent on a programmatic attack on Judaism."[34]

The prologue (1:1–8) derives its character from what follows. That is, the work and fate of John, as already observed, serve as a mirror to the work and fate of Jesus. As Elijah redivivus and precursor, John derives his importance from messianic prophecies (1:2–3) and the fulfillment in Jesus to which John is, after the event, increasingly conformed. Just as John's arrest in 1:14 is not recorded by Mark for its political but its christological interest, the prologue puts John forward, down to details of food and dress, as the messianic forerunner.

It must be conceded to Marxsen that *evangelion* (gospel)—not only in Mark 1:1, but in all its occurrences in Mark (1:14–15, 10:29, 13:10, 14:9)—derives from the evangelist.[35] Marxsen succeeds in showing that Matthew adopts the word from Mark, but gives it an entirely different sense (i.e., the separate "sermons" in Matthew become "gospels" preached by Jesus), while Luke historicizes in a way leading him to avoid the term *evangelion* (except in a derived way in the verb *evangelizesthai*). Paul preaches Christ, focusing on the cross, in a conceptual-theological fashion. Mark, also focusing on the cross, not only through the centrality of the Passion story but also through the device of the Secret within the pre-Passion introduction, preaches Christ by means of a "visual" representation of the Jesus tradition. For both Paul and Mark, "Christ himself is the gospel." Thus Mark 1:1, "gospel of Jesus Christ," being both objective and subjective genitive, means, "gospel which is Jesus Christ."

We are now prepared to observe and characterize the total scope of Mark's program. Conzelmann has put it like this:

His contribution consists not, therefore, in that he built non-messianic pieces into the framework of christological belief, but that he puts together in accord with the kerygma (understood in the sense of the Secret christology) a mass of christologically understood material. The idea of the Secret does not arise from historical-pragmatic considerations. It is rather an expression of a positive concept of revelation, as comprehended, for example, in the passage edited by Mark himself, Mk 4:10–12.

Not the unmessianic character of the units of the tradition, but on the contrary, the messianic ones cause the evangelist concern, in view of which he must by all means execute his theological program with sufficient care.[36]

Koester, speaking of the outcome of the long and arduous research of the Messianic Secret as Mark's characteristic feature in composing the Gospel, makes the same essential affirmation: "The solution is obvious today. Mark's tradition, the stories of the Divine Man and Messiah Jesus, was subjected to the principle of the cross; thus the 'secret' revelation of Jesus in his miracles."[37] The distinctiveness of Mark's work has been expressed by Eduard Schweizer in this manner: "Mark was the first to write a Gospel, and in so doing he created an entirely new literary form."[38] To this must be added from Conzelmann: "The Secret theory is the hermeneutical presupposition of the genre 'Gospel.' "[39]

Conzelmann's caveat that "the idea of the Secret does not arise from historical-pragmatic considerations" is addressed to Wrede's idea of Mark's fusion between messianic and nonmessianic materials. Political intentions could also be included under the term "pragmatic," and we must again make clear in this regard that in no instances where the political apology of Mark is supposed to have found its special expression (e.g., in the Passion narrative) do we encounter simultaneously his theory of concealment. This leads us to ask, in a more concrete way: What is the "positive concept of revelation" underlying Mark's Secret, and how is this evidenced in the Markan redaction? To answer this, we turn to Mark's "central section" (8:27–10:52) where the Secret is very decisively at play and where it is possible to see the polemical concerns of Mark in full swing.

The King That Didn't Reign

Albert Schweitzer branded the work of Wrede "thorough-going scepticism." This reaction rested primarily on Schweitzer's conservative position on the question of the messianic conscious-ness of Jesus, a position obviously untenable if Wrede's explana-tion of the Messianic Secret was valid. Schweitzer insisted that everything in the claims of Christianity hinged on Jesus' belief that he was the Messiah.[40] This is indeed a strange position on the part of one so famous as Schweitzer was for shattering time-honored positions of orthodoxy. It must be made clear, on the contrary, that this same attitude has frequently been held by those who decree that all the claims of Christianity rest on a biological virgin birth, a photographable rising of Jesus' body and its ascent into outer space, or on some other facet of belief that the person making such a statement regards as indispensable to his conception of Christianity. It should further be observed that what Jesus thought about himself should not be considered equivalent, either historically or theologically, with what the church affirms about him. The church obviously affirms Jesus to be the Christ. That is what Mark affirms from Mark 1:1 forward. It is apparent, however, that the affirmation "Jesus is the Christ" had effected a monumental change of language, a change that is epitomized in the central section of Mark when Jesus "rejects" Peter's confession, Mark 8:31–33, and attaches to the ordinary meaning of the word "Messiah" (Christ) a sense that was dis-covered in the church only after the crucifixion.

It must be reemphasized that Mark 8:30, "And he charged them to tell no one about him," does not mean that herein Jesus corroborates Peter's splendid insight, "You are the Christ" (8:29). What we meet in 8:30 is Mark's editorial trademark. Since

8:30, furthermore, is the bridge to what follows in verses 31–9:1, one naturally concludes that Mark's special concern lies in the very domain already suggested: the shaping of the (already existing) confession (represented in Peter) into a meaning that that confession, formed by ideas of political messianism, could not embrace. This means that Mark's polemical concern is to confront the false triumphalism found in the Hellenistic traditions of the "divine man" who meets with consummate mastery all the cosmic forces of evil, and the false triumphalism of the ethnic messiah (10:42) ruling with royal dominance over friend and foe alike, with the demand of the cross. Mark therefore gives to Christian confession a distinct ethical stamp. His Secret plants in the middle of the disciples' obtuseness and noncomprehension what we can call moral understanding. He not only proclaims Christ who is the gospel, but warns against the moral distortion that, he knows, already runs rife in the church. In this sense Mark's "program" is remarkably similar to that of Paul in 1 Corinthians, where Paul must make clear that the gospel of "Christ crucified" stands against the enthusiastic individualism of the fractious Corinthians. Before turning to that similarity more directly, it is necessary to indicate further the alteration espoused by Mark in the meaning of Messiah.

Considering the life of Jesus as a whole, it does not fit the definition of Messiah as that term was used in the time before Easter. As Bultmann puts it:

Moreover the synoptic tradition leaves no doubt about it that *Jesus' life and work* measured by traditional messianic ideas *was not messianic.* . . . Actually, "Messiah" was the term for the eschatological ruler; the word means "the Anointed" and came to mean simply "king." But it was not as a king, but as a prophet and a rabbi that Jesus appeared—and, one may add, as an exorcist. Nothing of the might and glory, which according to Jewish supposition would characterize the Messiah, was realized in Jesus' life—not in his exorcisms, for example, nor in his other mighty works. For though miracles were indeed a characteristic of the messianic period in Jewish belief, still the Messiah himself was not thought of as a miracle worker.[41]

Instead of the traditional view that Jesus must have thought, "I am the Messiah," it should be considered, against Schweitzer and books like *The Passover Plot* to which Jesus' messianic consciousness is the integral presupposition, what a positive embarrassment to Christianity this would actually be.[42] This is because the word Messiah in Jesus' time implied both political and military nationalism, embracing the "might and glory" emphasized above by Bultmann.

A glimpse of this can be had from the Song of Victory in the Qumran War Scroll where God, the "Valiant One" (following Dupont-Sommer's analysis), prevails with unchallengeable violence over all ethnic enemies:

> Arise, O Valiant One!
> Lead away Thy captives, O glorious Man!
> Do Thy plundering, O Valorous One!
> Set Thy hand upon the neck of Thine enemies
> and Thy foot upon the heap of the slain!
> Strike the nations Thy enemies
> And let Thy sword devour guilty flesh!
> Fill the land wilth glory
> And Thine inheritance with blessing!
> A multitude of cattle in Thy pastures,
> silver and gold and precious stones in Thy palaces!
> O Zion, rejoice greatly!
> Appear amid shouts of joy, O Jerusalem!
> Show yourselves, O all you cities of Judah!
> Open [thy] gat[es] for ever
> for the riches of the nations to enter in!
> And let their kings serve thee
> and let all thy oppressors bow down before thee
> and [let them lick] the dust [of thy feet]![43]

This song does not use the word Messiah, but it must be remembered that in the Rule of the Congregation, also from Qumran, "the anointed one of Israel" seats himself before "the commanders of Israel's thousands," that is, as the martial dignitary.[44] If, as seems a reasonable deduction, the sectarian expectations with

respect to the Messiah of Israel are conformable to their expectations with respect to God (as, indeed, in Christianity, Christ
is the "exegesis" of God, cf. John 1:18), the Song of Victory does
not leave much to the imagination as to what the martial Messiah shall accomplish.

It can, then, be said that the theological premise for Schweitzer's insistence on the messianic consciousness of Jesus is untenable. It can also be opposed on exegetical grounds as well.

It has been maintained that Jesus transformed the word Messiah along the lines of Isaiah 52:13–53:12, but neither in Mark
nor in Q is this passage utilized in connection with Jesus. Jesus'
identification with that section of Isaiah arose within the Christian community and is first attested in Luke 22:37. Matthew 8:17
uses Isaiah 53:4 to explicate not the suffering of Jesus but his
works of healing.[45] We have seen in the previous section that
in Matthew 12:17–21 is introduced a passage on the Isaianic
Servant (Isaiah 42:1–4) resulting from a misinterpretation or a
derived interpretation of the Secret idea in Mark 3:12. The
predictions of the Passion in Mark 8:31, 9:31, and 10:33–34 are
predictions after the event and shaped by the evangelist out of the
Passion material that is the basis for his Gospel. The suffering
assuredly propounded in Mark 8:31–9:1 does not employ Isaiah
52:13–53:12 and is distinctively molded by the Markan polemic
against a falsified christology.

Mark 14:62 (Jesus' response to the high priest) does not
furnish proof of the messianic consciousness of Jesus. B. H.
Streeter correctly argued that the original text of Mark 14:62 is
to be found in Matthew and Luke.[46] In these parallels, the question of the high priest, "Are you the Christ?," is answered by,
"You have said so" (Matt. 26:64), and "You say that I am"
(Luke 22:70). These parallels do not attest an agreement of Matthew and Luke against Mark, but are due to accidents of textual
transmission. That is, Matthew and Luke represent a text that
existed earlier in Mark 14:62 and was emended in the direction

of an explicit messianic confession by Jesus, "I am," while the original reading in Mark is still to be found in textual variants, especially Codex Koridethianus, which has, "You say that I am."

We have attempted to show that Mark, a book of Secret epiphanies, a Passion narrative with an extended introduction, is not only the first and unique *evangelion*, but it re-presents Christ in such a way as to counter a false messianic triumphalism that he discerned at work in the Christian community of his time. The "positive concept of revelation" that signals Mark's work is the moral understanding with which he informs Christian confession. In so far as Messiah was comprehended in terms of a political deliverer, Mark is not only nonpolitical, he is apolitical, for the Christ Mark presents stands in diametrical opposition to the conventional messianic hope. We must now corroborate this aspect of Mark's purpose by further explorations of the setting of his distinctive ideas.

Messianic Secret and Moral Understanding

If Mark, like Paul, proclaims a Christ crucified as the substance of the Gospel, it might prompt an immediate objection to connect the message of Mark with the issue of moral understanding. We are presently so imbued with Luther's restatement of faith justification, as that has come down to us through contemporary Christian existentialism, that the mere mention of morality is taken by some as a disservice to faith. Against this apprehension the hope may be expressed that there is still a distinguishable difference between morality and moralisms and that neither in Paul nor in the Gospels has the ethical enterprise of Christianity been reduced to a state of peonage by a kind of theological imperialism sometimes discovered in Paul's letters. It is appropriate

to remember in connection with Paul that his disavowal of antinomian euphoria (e.g., Romans 6) is as unmistakable as his
mandate for Christian freedom. It is undeniable that Paul's
counterposing of gospel and law (under which one may subsume
morality) was controlled by the situation to which he addressed
himself, as was equally true of Luther's scene. But the same
dialectic exists in Paul as we encounter in the problem of rule
and revolution. The course of revolution inexorably moves toward
the creation of a new rule, and the meaning of revolution is not
known until that law it creates has come into view. The following
may serve to illustrate the parallel between Mark and Paul in
this respect and to validate the focus upon moral understanding as
integral to Mark's program.

The "parties" or factions of 1 Corinthians 1:11–12 must
have been virulent ones to have spawned the amount of controversy that has marked the commentators' efforts to explain
what they were.[47] Conzelmann may represent a mediating viewpoint in saying that in the Corinthian correspondence Paul is
dealing not with Jews and resurgent Judaism in the church, but
with a Christian religiosity of the Hellenistic type.[48] The Corinthian enthusiasm grew out of a *gnōsis* (knowledge) that claimed
transcendent freedom: "We all have knowledge" (1 Cor. 8:1);
"all things are lawful" (1 Cor. 6:12, 10:23). The Corinthians have
"already" (1 Cor. 4:8), so they believed, experienced on the other
side of judgment the promised eschatological gifts and thus enjoy
an existence that is not only "beyond" eschatology, but beyond
the moral struggle that attends those who have not yet reached
such a state.[49] Wilckens may be correct in affirming that behind
the "wisdom" of the Corinthians (e.g., 1 Cor. 1:17) lurks a teaching on baptism that found in the sacrament only the acquisition
of the triumphal benefits of the exalted Christ and nothing of the
existence for the baptized designated by the crucified Christ.[50] It
will continue to be a matter of dispute how far developed at
Corinth was the gnostic thought against which Paul fulminates.

But there is broad agreement as to Paul's method of dealing with the false enthusiasm of the "gnostic problem" at Corinth. It is the theology of the cross thematically expressed in 1 Corinthians 1:23, a remedy that, as Conzelmann urges, has profound ethical import: "one has to work out the relation of gift and demand (ethic). When the end of the tension between these two is proclaimed, I can understand that only as enthusiasm. With Paul, the 'imperative' of God's demand is never absorbed by the "indicative' of the communication of salvation. Otherwise, the 'indicative' itself would become law."[51]

Knigge has spoken of the uniqueness of Mark's theology in a manner quite applicable to what has been said of Paul: "Marcan thinking is defined by a *theologia crucis* which is completely of his own formulation. The cross appears not only as the crisis of human thinking and notions (I Cor. 1:18–31), but is also the hermeneutical key to understanding the revelation of God in Jesus Christ."[52] Eduard Schweizer adds to these remarks very clear judgments on the ethical consequences of Mark's joining together of the triumphal journey of Christ through the world (as represented, for example, in the kerygma of 1 Timothy 3:16) and the story of Jesus that tells of his struggle and death. Mark's placing together of the historical Jesus and the kerygma was his way of resisting the gnostic use to which the kerygma was already being subjected and disclosing to the believer what discipleship actually means. Schweizer concludes:

Is then the importance of the historical Jesus merely ethical? As soon as we realize that ethics are not a mere appendix to faith, but that, on the contrary, faith cannot be lived except ethically, that is, in the wholeness of our life, in our thinking and speaking, feeling and acting, it is clear that such a formulation would not reduce this importance. But, maybe, it is wiser to avoid a term which is so much discussed.[53]

Again, Keck has given essentially the same characterization of Mark's work in the following passage:

The subtlety of Mark's work does not lie in imaginative allusions to the supposed myth of the secret savior but in the way he has taken up the *theios anēr* [divine man] materials and restricted their significance by interpreting the life of Jesus as a whole in the light of the cross, both that borne by Jesus and that borne by the disciples—a theme absent from the gnostic myth. Mark's theology is indeed in tension with the *theios anēr* materials, . . . and Mark's tension with it is not derived from the myth but his insistence on the necessity of suffering for the Son of Man and his disciples.[54]

Neither in the case of Paul and the Corinthians nor in the case of Mark and those for whom he wrote the Gospel can it be determined unambiguously what exact conditions evoked the "theology of the cross" with its moral implications. One is drawn for this reason to speak less specifically of "the gnostic problem" as the common denominator of the two theologies and to speak instead of "the human problem." Thus Peter's protestation against the Passion in Mark 8:32, with its clear overtones of ethnic triumphalism and self-assertion, has more in common with the problem of violence than the antinomian euphoria of the Corinthian troublemakers, but the mutual basis on which both aberrations rest is implied by the single remedy proclaimed in both situations.

This can be further clarified by referring to the prophetic background of Mark's special polemic on the lack of understanding among the disciples and, in particular, to the Markan parable theory in 4:10–12. We begin with the latter.

Without resorting to retranslations into Aramaic and other devices designed to overcome the obvious sense of the purpose clause in Mark 4:12, Mark seems to say that the parable produces a misunderstanding the consequence of which is damnation. The Hebrew *māshāl* (aphorism, parable, allegory) is used at some places in Old Testament literature in parallel with *ḥidāh,* meaning "riddle" or "perplexing saying."[55] Ezekiel 17:2 states, for example, "Son of man, propound a riddle (*ḥidāh*), and speak an

allegory (*māshāl*) to the house of Israel." Then follows (verses
3–10) the allegory of the eagles, designed to expound in its complex if not abstruse manner the convenantal unfaithfulness of
Judah resulting in political disaster. Similarly in Psalm 49:4, "I
will incline my ear to a proverb (*māshāl*); I will solve my riddle
(*ḥidāh*) to the music of the lyre," the question with which the
Psalmist wrestles, his "riddle," is the time of trouble, the life
of insecurity before the "Pit." As Ezekiel sounds the characteristic
prophetic note (Ezek. 16:49, "Behold, this was the guilt of your
sister Sodom: she and her daughter had pride, surfeit of food, and
prosperous ease, but did not aid the poor and needy"), lambasting
the moral and economic arrogance of Jerusalem, so the Psalmist
(Ps. 49:5–20) wrestles in his riddle with the pomp of the rich and
mighty.[56]

Since Isaiah 6:9–10 underlies Mark's unusual thought in the
editorial section, Mark 4:10–12, the thought of Isaiah may throw
light on Mark's Secret theme.[57] Among the prophets, the word that
was meant for life and healing was "so misunderstood and rejected
because of people's sin and ignorance, that it became in fact an
instrument of judgment and condemnation (cf., e.g., Isa. 28:13,
Jer. 23:29)."[58] Isaiah's call, reflectively narrated in exactly these
terms in Isaiah 6, presupposes with irony that the encounter with
impenitence is to be so pervasive that it must be written, so to
speak, into the seer's "contract." And, by the ancient theological
rationale, the consequence of the preachment (unheeded prophecy
leads to no repentance, which leads to judgment and exile) is
described as its intention and purpose.

It must be faced that Mark in 4:10–11 distinguishes between
"insiders" and "outsiders," as if to suggest that appeal to the
prophets' dilemma of human hardness and impenitence is not
applied to those "inside" but only those "outside." This is, however, another example of the imperfect execution of the editorial
program, for in the section 8:14–21 (verses 17–18 in particular)
Isaiah 6:9–10 again is applied to the problem of noncomprehen-

sion, this time with respect to the disciples themselves. It is also obvious in Mark's handling of Peter's confession that the disciples fail the test of moral understanding. This feature may be ascribed to an editorial inconsistency, but, at the same time, it delivers Mark from an inclination toward apocalyptic sectarianism and draws his redaction into the orbit of prophetic ethicism, as the following indicates.

In the Manual of Discipline from Qumran, all creation is attributed to the "God of knowledge" (1QS iii:5). Though the divine order of creation is secret, God reveals it to those chosen for his convenant. In the Hymn Scroll (1QH), this is referred to as the "marvelous mysteries" (*raze pele'*). IQH x:2–5 emphasizes that man, unaided, is wholly incapable of understanding these mysteries: "None can understand thy laws and none gaze upon mysteries. . . ." But the hymnist exults, "This I have known from thy understanding, for thou hast opened my ear for the marvelous mysteries" (1QH i:21). In 1QS xi:3–8 it also reflects upon the hiddenness of God's mysteries and the privilege of those appointed for enlightenment:

Far from the wellspring of his knowledge he has opened up my light and my eye has seen his wonderful works . . . and from the source of his righteousness [come] the precepts of light in my heart, through his marvelous mysteries my eye has gazed upon the eternal being: a saving knowledge which is hidden from the man of knowledge, a wise insight [which is hidden from] the sons of men. . . . Of the company of flesh God gave this knowledge as an eternal possession to those whom he has chosen and allowed them to share in the lot of the holy ones, and with the sons of heaven he joined their fellowship in the council of the Community.[59]

Mark's distinction between the bafflement of parables to those outside and the privileged enlightenment imparted to those inside (e.g., Mark 1:21, 7:17–18, 9:28, 10:10) has nuances akin to the sectarian view of enlightenment, knowledge, and salvation, right down to the unsavory "double predestination" of Mark 4:12 whereby the outsiders are given over to perdition by divine decree meted out beforehand. The Persian loan word *rāz* (secret or mystery) occurring in the Dead Sea Scrolls was already fixed in the vocabulary of apocalypse by its use in the Book of Daniel (e.g., Dan. 2:17–30). There again are found the enlightened ones (*maskilim*, Dan. 11:33, 35, 12:3, 10), called variously by the translators "the wise" or "teachers," who, like Daniel, are "in the know" with respect to the eschatological mysteries, the unfolding of the End, and the rise and fall of political powers.

Schubert is content to call the Qumran idea of secrecy/ revelation and enlightened elite "Jewish gnosticism," while cautioning that the scrolls do not posit a good, transcendent God versus an evil, creator God, or evidence an awareness of the divine spark of life in men that must be liberated from the prison of the world.[60]

This brief excursus indicates at least a shared fund of mystery terminology common to Mark, prophecy, apocalypse, and gnosticism. With regard to the gnostic idea, it should be recorded in addition to Paul's struggle at Corinth that the Gospel of Thomas (log. 13) contains a recognizable parallel to the "Who do men say that I am?" episode in Mark 8:27–30. Thomas surpasses both Peter and Matthew by refusing to compare Jesus with any other thing. To gnostic thought (echoing in this case the prohibition against images in the decalogue), comparisons (or parables?) cannot disclose the Father or the Son, because that violates the divine hiddenness. Logion 83 reads: "Jesus said: The images are manifest to man, and the light which is within them is hidden in the image of the light of the Father. He will be revealed and his image is concealed by his light."[61] Jesus, who is the image and effulgence of God (cf. Heb. 1:3; 2 Cor. 4:4) hides the image he is by the light of the Father in him. Thus Thomas affirms that no image (comparison) can suffice to disclose Jesus.

We must conclude that these ideas carry us outside the range of Markan ideas, despite enticing terminological parallels. Mark is, granting editorial inconsistencies, closer to the prophetic milieu. This conclusion is encouraged by the fact that the Gospel of Thomas (log. 55) also contains a saying on cross bearing, *which has no connection with the "confession of Thomas"* in logion 13. Even if we cannot yet conclude that the Gospel of Thomas represents a tradition of the sayings of Jesus independent of or prior to the Markan tradition, Thomas illustrates the ability of religious thought to separate the very elements that give Mark (and all the Gospels) its catalytic force when they are brought together. This same quality of Mark's redaction neutralizes even those gestures occasionally present in Mark toward sectarian appocalypticism. Even in the passage Mark 6:33–8:26, where, if our argument on pp. 80 ff. holds, an entire section has been brought together under the banners of Isaiah 35:5–6 and the "enlightenment" motif, Mark "ethicizes" by bringing the disciples themselves under the stricture of "hardness" (6:52, 8:17–18). So Mark plays no sectarian game.

In the *Theology of Culture*, Paul Tillich traces the genius of the prophetic idea.[62] It is what he calls the struggle between the "God of time" and the "God of space." The prophetic vindication of the God of time has its inception in the Abrahamic covenant when it states, "in you shall all nations be blessed." Among the prophets is encountered the righteous God who cannot be conformed to the goals and interests of the particular people but lets his judgment fall even upon the chosen. This God wrestles in the prophets with the ethnic God, the God of space. He overcomes. This it is that distinguishes the greatness of the prophets and leads every one of the spokesmen for the God of time to grief and isolation, to the ironic lamentation of Isaiah 6:9–10. If it be said that "The Zealots stood in true succession to the Jahwist prophets of old,"[63] it can be seen that this was indeed that brand of ethnic prophecy that constituted the virulent adversary against which an Amos or an Isaiah had to enter the lists, and the correct response to such a claim would be:

... from the view of nationalistic self-interest, the prophets were *traitors*, and were often so regarded by many of their contemporaries. . . . It is extremely important for Brandon's case that he scotch the notion that Jesus restored prophetism . . . it is precisely the prophetic image of Jesus which most stands in the way of the acceptance of his view, and only by denying its basis can he destroy its appeal.[64]

Summary

We have looked at Mark in panoramic fashion as a book of Secret epiphanies, a Passion narrative with an extended introduction. Mark's structure has been set forth in such a way as to explicate the editorial task that the evangelist discharged. It has been shown that in the details of the Markan Gospel, where the evangelist's hand is discernedly at work, the ingredients of a political apology are not to be found. On the contrary, when Mark brings into catalytic fusion the sagas of the divine man and the tradition of the Passion under the agency of the Messianic Secret, creating a literary form without precedent or successor, the *theologia gloriae* is transmuted by distinct ethical elements into the *theologia crucis* (Mark 10:42–45). This is not a creation of Mark, but he presents it in a unique, unrepeated fashion. Mark does not work from materials that compel him to synthesize the nonmessianic Jesus of history with the Christ extolled in the church. He must, rather, inform the belief of the church with the kind of moral understanding that would give the christological confession strength against its inclination to antinomian euphoria. The Secret motif is not, therefore, a religious hoax sanctified by the rewards that history placed upon Mark's undertaking, but a positive concept of revelation by means of which Mark, in line with what the traditional materials already indicated, deethnicized and depoliticized the meaning of Messiah.

Mark's design of discipleship upon the model of the cross can only signify a setting in which the addressees are faced with an intense struggle to maintain the integrity of faith. This could have been due to aberrant developments within the church itself as well as persecutions or severities imposed from the outside. Marxsen has attempted to relate the situation of Mark to the hegira of Christians from Jerusalem about A.D. 68, as indicated in the tumultuous tribulations of Mark 13. While this setting cannot now be proved or disproved, it has the advantage of suggesting at least the kind of plight familiar to Mark. Mark soberly recognizes where Christ and the church stand with respect to the structures of power, whether in Rome or Jerusalem. There are in Mark no awkward postures of affected civility between Christ and Caesar, because experience (both of Jesus and the church) has exposed the falsity of such a thing.

In a period when men tend to assign to all phenomena a political significance, either overt or hidden, it is only with much caution that one can address political questions to a literature which does not share this panpolitical outlook. There is an attitude in both prophetic and apocalyptic thought, carried over into the Gospels, that we may define as "beyond politics." The cultural optimism that encourages men to think that the most serious problems submit to political solution is not one frequently expressed in biblical thought. This does not mean there is no basis in the Gospel for civic responsibility or political action. It does mean that such responsibility and action are discharged under an awareness of the limits to which human institutions are subject. This will become clear as we attempt now to bring the figure of the non-Zealot Jesus into dialogue with the contemporary problem of violence.

V. JESUS AND VIOLENCE

In the preceding three chapters indications have been given of
the difficulties faced in trying to establish a line of direct, unmediated communication with the historical Jesus concerning
contemporary problems. This does not mean, however, that there
is no valid basis on which the subject Jesus and violence can be
investigated. With particular reference to the Gospel of Mark,
we have found that there is a theology of the cross that brought
the figure of Jesus out of the clouds, so to speak, and set it in
relationship to men and the human situation, conveying a type
of moral understanding. This moral understanding is implicit in
discipleship. It *is* discipleship.

   This does not mean that morality is to be distilled from
theology as the permanent and valid part that remains after the
trappings of doctrine and talk about God have been laid to rest.
It means rather that theology itself embraces an understanding to
be defined as ethical. When placed, therefore, in its proper context, the subject, Jesus and violence, means the consideration of
violence from the standpoint of that kind of moral understanding
that the Christian gospel expresses.

Moral Understanding

By "understanding" is meant the comprehension that man has of himself and the world under the auspices of the Gospel, namely, that he is the undeserving recipient of the grace God imparts through Jesus Christ. This understanding is to be contrasted with all forms of self-righteousness by which man seeks, independently of the Gospel, to establish his acceptability. It is thus distinguished from notions of pride, success, competence, power or their opposites, in so far as both power and impotence, success and failure, pride and humiliation, competence and incompetence are considered as lying within the domain of the self and its doings as opposed to God's acceptance of men through Christ.

While it is conceivable such understanding of one's self, manifested in thanksgiving, is possible outside the Gospel—the Spirit blows where it wills—what is theoretically possible must not be confused with what is actually experienced. This does not imply that Christian belief has conducted or expects to conduct some kind of experiment in self-understanding designed to show that its product has a measured superiority over what men experience in Buddhism, Islam, Secularism, Humanism, or whatever. The measurement of such products would be as impossible as the devising of agreeable terms on which such a calculation could be made. Faith would also in this fashion seek to prop itself up by proofs that in themselves belie the unmerited grace on which faith claims to rest.

The experience of grace is the ground of discipleship and the basis of the social relationship. For this reason, particularly in the present theological situation, we must speak of the Gospel in terms of moral understanding, if the biblical focus of Christianity is to be retained. This is necessary in our time, because the understanding created by the Gospel is compromised, on the one hand, by an individualistic and subjective preoccupation with the self and, on the other hand, by the misuse of the psychology of adjustment.

Self-understanding, by virtue of what it means to be human, is social in nature. George H. Mead gave classical expression to this, particularly when he traced the genesis of the self to the use of language, communication, and the symbols of human intercourse.[1] Self is a reflexive, relational term.

In biblical thought the social character of human beings is centrally expressed in theological language, that is, in relation to God and the people of God, while the perimeter of neighborly concern is being pushed constantly outward, as in the Parable of the Good Samaritan (Luke 10:29–37). Our discussion has revealed that we do not meet in the Gospels Jesus "in himself," but Jesus as grasped within and mediated by the church. The community narrates the history of Jesus in the light of its own history. Since Paul had no direct dealings with the historical Jesus, Luke's record of "Why do you persecute me?" addressed to Paul in Acts 9:4 ("me" referring to Jesus) can only mean "Why do you persecute the church?" Likewise, when Matthew 9:8 uses the plural noun "men" to expound the singular "Son of man" in Matthew 9:6, it is only a striking example of the interplay between the one and the many that is encountered everywhere in the biblical message.

The consequence of this is that there is no proper understanding of the self either in psychology or religion that does not also embrace the societal aspect of existence. Times of social disaster drive faith into personalistic and subjective forms of expression. This development reflects, therefore, the impact of despair. In some of its manifestations, Christian existentialism has encouraged this trend, and thus formed in its social and moral outlook a strange coalition with pietism of the Billy Graham type. These approaches compromise the basic social character of man and summon us to an understanding that distorts the ethical aspect of religion.

The same forces are at work in the psychology of adjustment, and this also impedes the kind of moral understanding that emerges from the theology of the cross. Adjustment does imply a social awareness, but here the problem consists in the way the corporate life is conceived and the relation of the self to it. The problem can be illustrated from the world of education.

In the 1960s, education was rocked by deep changes in student attitudes brought about by traumatic and violent happenings in social experience. This phenomenon was not just an American affair (to which our subsequent remarks are mainly confined), but was broadspread throughout the world. The student mood, furthermore, did not lack faculty counterparts and was, in some respects, a fructification of ideas long present but relatively neglected in the intellectual world.

In his study *Political Violence*, H. L. Nieburg lists the factors that increased the incidence of violence in America during the sixties: 1) the rapidity and magnitude of social change, uprooting of populations, obsolescence of existing institutions in dealing with these forces; 2) war and diplomacy that legitimize violence and intensify social control by formal restraints; 3) the Vietnam war; and 4) the black revolution.[2] Among these, he singles out the last one as "the active ingredient and most salient precipitant of violence." Educational institutions have frequently been aware of the factors listed by Nieburg, for it is the specific province of many departments of learning to bring them under investigation. Awareness has grown that no part of the culture remains unaffected by the causes of violence, and education itself, as the student movements have been effective in disclosing, has been unveiled in its role as ally of the military-industrial complex. The training of students for efficient and successful functioning in the professions or social structures as now constituted commands a diminishing amount of enthusiasm in all educational institutions. Disturbed and guilt-stricken by the magnitude of violence, students demand new and experimental forms of vocational life by which they can become effective agents of needed change.

This is no less the case in theological education. The minister as counselor who deals therapeutically with the anxieties and frustrations of persons within existing institutions has a receding prominence. It is felt, rather, that the institutions as now constituted, including the church, are causative rather than corrective factors in the incidence of violence. Consequently the design of the minister as an agent of social change is increasingly sought.

This alteration in the concept of the church's ministry had come into being in part because the theories of psychotherapy that shaped the role of pastoral psychology have also felt the impact of violent social forces transcending the issues of individual adjustment. Fromm asks:

Is the alienated person with little love and little sense of identity not better adapted to the technological society of today than a sensitive, deeply feeling person? When speaking of health in a sick society, one uses the concept of health in a sociological sense, as denoting adaptation to society. The real problem here is precisely that of the conflict between "health" in human terms and "health" in social terms; a person may function well in a sick society precisely because he is sick in human terms.[3]

Moral understanding implies, therefore, that the wholeness of persons does not consist in their ability to perform happily within the culture; it embraces, beyond that, their contribution to the social sanity that liberates the culture from its drift toward violence. This by no means implies that the therapy of persons loses its weight in the tasks of Christian ministry. It does mean that the concept of healing is altered, as well as the measurement of its effectiveness. Applied to the problems of industrial production, there can be no doubt that various forms of group psychology can result in an increase of output and reduction of discomfort along the line of production. But there are increasing numbers of people who simply do not want to spend their lives making more napalm.

For decades we have been assured that "changed persons will bring about a changed society." Whether this axiom is pronounced by the old or the new forms of pietism, the results remain the same. The institutional violence inherent in racism, poverty, and war does not come seriously under the purview of what is understood by "changed."

Violence and Moral Understanding

As we turn to the specific correlation of the problem of violence and moral understanding, the issue is scarcely one of ends. We assume that all want violence eliminated and the creation of a nonviolent society. No war, no revolution, and few acts of individual violence have been engaged in except with the intent of rectifying intolerable conditions and establishing thereby more equitable forms of order and peace.[4] Obviously, as Washington carried out in Southeast Asia what proved to be a highly violent form of Communist containment, it was done with the public assurance that this was necessary for the future peace of Asia. As violence mounted on the home front among the civil rights activists and the peace activists, it was explained as the only effective recourse in a situation that had proved itself impervious to other (nonviolent) forms of redress. We approach a world, as Orwell warned, in which violence and destruction mean peace and order. The discussion comes thus to be one of means and not of ends.

To intensify awareness of where the points of basic disagreement actually are, two examples will be used, one from Eduard Schweizer and one from Reinhold Niebuhr.

In the previous chapter, we drew upon Schweizer's treatment of Mark, especially his view that Mark ethicized the kerygma by joining it to the narratives of Jesus' life and teaching and relating the theology of the cross to the life of discipleship. Schweizer has nothing to say in this connection, however, about nonviolence. In fact, Schweizer joined others in the Swiss Evangelical Church Federation in 1958 to defeat a resolution backed by Karl Barth that would have placed preparation for atomic warfare in irreconcilable conflict with the Christian faith. According to John Yoder, Schweizer, with the majority, refused to repudiate atomic weapons on principle, because the church lacked the authority "to settle such technical military matters."[5] Schweizer is a former student of Bultmann. It also happens that in 1958 Bultmann published an important article, "Theology for Freedom and Responsibility," that sets forth in concise terms his view of the theological and moral task of the church at that time. The position espoused in this article sounds so much like the Schweizer argument on nuclear arms that the passage is quoted for observation:

To some Christians the church's competence to make political judgments appears to arise from the fact that the church must after all condemn war under all circumstances. True as this is, the competence of the church to make political judgments does not follow from it. For the church can and must inculcate in all men their responsibility for seeing to it that matters do not come to war. But how can a war be prevented in this or that specific case—this is a political question, one which the church cannot judge and decide. Simply to cry "Never more war!" accomplishes nothing.[6]

We must briefly recapitulate the history of this period.[7] In 1934, the Confessional Church of Germany had sounded the alarm on the totalitarian encroachments of National Socialism, the party of Hitler, by publishing the Barmen Confession.[8] Now heralded as a courageous and prophetic example of Christian social witness, the Barmen statement could not command, even within the church, the kind of support necessary to bring Nazi ideology to a halt. After the war, West Germany under Konrad Adenauer and the Christian Democrats, with substantial American aid, was brought into the strategy of Communist containment, joined NATO, and began to rearm. Martin Niemoeller (with Karl Barth's backing) and others from the Barmen group, though by no means all of them, opposed West Germany's rearmament and her inclusion in NATO on the premise that these moves laid the ground for World War III in Europe, a war to be fought with nuclear weapons and pitting East and West Germany against one another. In March 1958, these issues were joined in the Synod of the Evangelical Church when a petition focusing primarily on the outlawing of nuclear weapons and Christian participation in preparation for nuclear war was presented over the signatures of 364 West German Protestants, mostly clergymen.

It is in this context of events that we must understand Bultmann's dictum that how a specific war can be prevented is "a political question." This strongly resembles Schweizer's warning that the settlement of technical military matters does not lie in the church's authority. In both the Swiss and the German situation, the Bultmannian position prevailed.

The inadequacy of this position has already been suggested, first, on the premise that it falsely privatizes and individualizes the nature of religious belief and moral understanding. One feels in the Bultmannian judgment of the matter a heavy influence from the Lutheran idea of the two spheres of church and state with "no trespass" signs placed at strategic places. The paradox we already face is that of a church that condemns war and preaches peace while it remains ready all the while to lend its moral support to war once the political decision has been made.

The Christian majority has thus so memorialized the virtues of soldiery that Bultmann's view that "the church must after all condemn war under all circumstances" envisions a message that never seems to come through to the people. Even among the Barmen confessors, no strong disposition was evidenced that draft-age Christians, once the political decision for war had been made, should refuse participation. Even Niemoeller, from prison, offered his services "in any capacity" to the German Navy when the war commenced.[9]

When we refer, second, to political decisions about peace or judgments about atomic weapons as belonging to a special political competence outside the authority of the church, it places around political decisions an aura of scientific sanctity and adequacy that does not in fact exist. We referred in the first chapter to the Bay of Pigs invasion and the expert opinion behind it, opposed only by Fulbright and Schlesinger. Unless we are willing to say that in governmental affairs only power, successfully applied, determines what is right, then we must discern that political judgments are choices between alternatives in which moral factors are present. The constant refrain of racist governments from Alabama to South Africa is that those in power know what the requirements of peace are and can keep the peace if the moralists do not stick their noses into government business. When Adolf Berle, as a professional governmental adviser, admits that President Truman on the question of the use of atomic weapons in 1945 was advised by "a committee of eminent but not too intelligent Americans," he explodes the groundless confidence that churchmen place in the competence of high councils of government. In this, they parallel the attitude of scientists who devote their knowledge to producing ever more sophisticated weapons, washing their hands of moral responsibility in the confidence that political authorities will safely manage that department. When in December 1938 Otto Hahn discovered the basic formula for atomic fission, the formula on which all subsequent atomic science including the atomic bomb was dependent, he adamantly refused to devote his science to military development.[10] The political effect of this commitment was minimal, however, as long as countless other scientists, encouraged by the example of churchmen, were prepared to let governmental experts decide whether atomic weapons were to be made and used. Today American science texts in the lower schools seldom mention Otto Hahn. The pages on atomic discoveries are devoted to the "great" scientists who helped build the bomb.

It can be said against Bultmann and Schweizer, in the third place, that letting the political technicians make the decisions about specific wars or weapons development constitutes a decision that is, in itself, pervasively political. We can well imagine what weight the moral opinion of the church (that matters must not come to war) will have, if governments know that in the final analysis the church will faithfully present arms once the decision for war has been made. By managing its definition of the area embraced by the political, the government knows in advance how far the counterforces among the people can be expected to carry their opposition. This is also the basis of propaganda and the withholding from the people, or even their representative bodies, of information that might weaken the credibility of the government's position. It is, therefore, a thoroughly political act when the church surrenders to the state's bid for autonomy in the decision to employ violence, and this applies to both internal and external policies of the state.

This may serve to explain, then, why we find Schweizer's emphasis on the nature of moral theology in the book of Mark correct, while we disagree with his efforts to apply this understanding to the question of nuclear arms and the nature of political authority.

Reinhold Niebuhr became a symbol of the American Christian majority from about 1940 onward. We have been arguing, in effect, that nonviolence as a positive expression of love is the salient feature of Christian moral understanding. Yet Niebuhr could write in 1940 that "There is not the slightest support in Scripture for this doctrine of non-violence."[11]

The context of Niebuhr's statement reveals its polemical character. Niebuhr was vigorously rooting out from the church the pacifist feelings that deterred America from entering the war for the defense of France and England before the advances of Hitler. Under the preaching of churchmen like Harry Emerson Fosdick, George A. Buttrick, and Ernest Fremont Tittle, Christian pacifism and internationalism had reached wide audiences within the church during the 1930s. Niebuhr was resolved to expose the untenability of the claims of pacifism and thus to secure support in the church for America's active engagement in the war against Germany.

In the same setting where he categorically denies any biblical basis for nonviolence, Niebuhr readily agrees that the teaching of Jesus, particularly the Sermon on the Mount, commands non-resistance. Thus nonviolence is a compromise, a diluting of the teaching of Jesus. This dilution shows that the pacifists are no more followers of the example and teaching of Jesus than Christians who accept, under conditions, the necessity of war as the lesser of two evils.

Niebuhr's strictures against "political pacifism," which assumed that unilateral disarmament and nonviolent resistance would inevitably bring about a reciprocal nonviolence by the enemy, were not inappropriate. Those who take the *theologia crucis* seriously as the basis of discipleship are certainly misinformed to found their position on the hopes of pragmatic success. That is the opposite of cross bearing. On the other hand, it cannot be conceded, when one views the totality of the ministry and teaching of Jesus, that there is nothing in it to provide the basis for nonviolence and the nonviolent resistance of evil. The Gospels are teeming with controversy. In Mark Jesus resists disease and disability, hypocrisy and cruelty. His resistance of evil gave the

tradition its aspect of cosmic, transcendental conflict and gave
rise to the classic idea of Christus Victor. One may say that
this portrayal is merely the way the evangelist chooses to put
the tradition, but the same could be said of the famous nonresistance text in Matthew 5:38–42, as it could be said of the unbridled
polemicism of Matthew 23. Whatever can be known of the historical circumstances surrounding the crucifixion, it hardly stands
to reason that matters came to this end if no occasion of offense
had been found on the part of Jesus' adversaries. Examination of
the pertinent Gospel passages reveals a Jesus who resisted
maximally, but within the limits imposed by his own doctrine of
love.

Virtually all advocates of nonviolence recognize the relativity
that lies in moral judgments and actions. When, therefore, the
effort is made to portray nonviolence in absolute terms, it is a
convenience of debate that does not correspond to the facts. In
respect to nonviolent resistance, it cannot be doubted that this
is something less than absolute or complete nonresistance. That
nonviolence is without the slightest support in Scripture is, however, a statement of fact that reading the Gospels does not support.

What Augustine was to the Roman emperorship, in providing
a theology of just war to cope with the political exigencies of the
fourth and fifth centuries, Reinhold Niebuhr was to President
Roosevelt in the undergirding of World War II with churchly
sanctions in 1941. The dominance of this theology is part of the
church's history to the present time, with consequences that
Niebuhr would perhaps himself disavow. As violence in both
internal and foreign affairs has mounted in frequency since 1945,
the church is deprived of confidence that either its understanding
or its practice corresponds to the design of Christ or the requirements of human need. This new situation has been brought about
in part by the fact that Reinhold Niebuhr, John C. Bennett,
and others of the *Christianity and Crisis* circle vigorously refused

to support the war in Vietnam. This leads to further considerations that weigh against the Niebuhrian consensus that prevailed after 1940, considerations further demonstrating the concrete relationship between moral understanding and the problem of violence.

In *Christ and Culture*, H. Richard Niebuhr set forth five types of answers to the problematical relationship between Christian faith and human civilization attested in Christian history. This work exemplified in the postwar period, just as Reinhold Niebuhr's had done in an earlier period, the moral and social orientation of the Christian majority.

Among the five types of answers that Christianity has given to the question of its relationship to culture (Christ against culture, Christ of culture, Christ above culture, Christ and culture in paradox, and Christ the transformer of culture), the first, Christ against culture, is the one most pertinent to this discussion. This is so not only because it establishes the terms upon which the other four typologies are constructed, but also because it belongs chronologically to the beginnings of Christianity and brings us into more immediate dialogue with the biblical period as our point of reference.

H. Richard Niebuhr finds that "Christ against culture" is "widely held to be the typical attitude of the first Christians."[12] It is illustrated from the First Letter of John, where "the world" as the "heir of Cain" (cf. 1 John 3:12) is "pagan society, with its sensuality, superficiality and pretentiousness, its materialism and its egoism" (C. H. Dodd). Niebuhr also finds in the "two ways" doctrine of the Didache, Hermas, Barnabas, and 1 Clement evidence of the first solution, Christ against culture. Tertullian (early third century) also represents this view, rejecting Christian participation in political life and refusing military duty to Christians, because Christ "in disarming Peter, unbelted every soldier" (Tertullian, *De Idololatria*, 19). Tolstoy held to this concept in more modern times, with his strenuous efforts to spell out in cultural rejection the literal meaning of Matthew 5. The

Mennonites exemplify this position most purely among the sects of Christianity, rejecting politics and the military and preserving their own customs in economics and education.

When H. Richard Niebuhr avers that Christ against culture is the view "widely held to be the typical attitude of the first Christians," he detaches himself from this viewpoint and expressly states that it is subject to question. What these questions are would perhaps lead Niebuhr into the kind of discussion we have pursued in chapters 2 through 4, in so far, at least, as it has to do with the teaching of the Gospels. Since we are prepared to agree with those who associate what Niebuhr calls "Christ against culture" with the early Christians, because the portrait of Jesus in the Gospels is one of nonviolence, we are prepared to formulate a primary objection to his delineation of Christ and culture.

The objection is this: Just as culture refers to the successive institutions and values of different historical epochs, Christ must root in a continuity with Christian beginnings. While Niebuhr intimates what those beginnings imply (i.e., Christ against culture), he does not seek to confirm this or to determine what place it occupies in giving the term Christ some coherent and continuous sense. The following can be added to this.

In *Christian Attitudes Toward War and Peace*, Roland Bainton clarifies the point left somewhat obscure by *Christ and Culture*. That is, in his tracing of the history of Christianity, Bainton finds that the early period beginning with the New Testament and continuing through the third century until the time of Constantine stood apart from war and the military life.[13] Bainton gives the reasons often enumerated for the church's abnegation of war, including expectation of the end of the world, the unacceptability of emperor worship and Roman religious rites connected with the military, and the otherworldly character of the church. He concludes, however, that "the primary ground of their aversion was the conviction of its incompatibility with love."[14]

Reinhold Niebuhr left no uncertainty as to his judgment about what the teaching of Jesus clearly implies, namely, non-resistance.[15] This is reintroduced here only to make clear the one point that Reinhold Niebuhr, if compelled to use the categories of *Christ and Culture*, would place Jesus under H. Richard Niebuhr's first type, Christ against culture. He would, further, concur in Bainton's assessment of the pre-Constantinian church, though on his terms the period before Constantine would have to be judged heretical because it was also pacifist.

When H. Richard Niebuhr wrote *The Responsible Self*, a book that in many respects consummates his distinguished intellectual career, the tendency we are now criticizing in *Christ and Culture* appeared in fuller form. That is, James Gustafson can point out in the introduction to *The Responsible Self* that the place of the New Testament is not treated in that book.[16] So Gustafson proceeds to glean from H. Richard Niebuhr's other writings the place that he assigns to the biblical witness. In this regard, H. Richard Niebuhr often sounded the alarm against biblicism, moralism, and fundamentalism, as most ethicists are prone to do. On the other hand, to emphasize our first objection, it should be self-evident that a church that surrenders its serious attention to the Jesus portrayed in the Gospels must constantly question what claim it can rightly make to the attributive Christian.

There are certainly a number of references to the New Testament in *The Responsible Self*. H. Richard Niebuhr wishes, through these allusions, to contrast what he classifies as the deontological (i.e., expressing obligation from some kind of biblical norm) ethic derived from the Bible by Bultmann and Barth and his own "responsible" ethic, in which the self responds to what God has done and is doing in the various situations that meet one. The difficulty in this approach is that, as Gustafson has said in connection with the ethic of Paul Lehmann, there are innumerable critical junctures of life in which one must honestly admit: "I

haven't the slightest idea what God is doing in this situation."[17]
Isaiah may have been able to say what God's hidden intention
was in the action of Israel's enemies, but few of us are prophets
with that kind of vision.[18] In the absence of such insight, we are
usually driven back to how God has acted (e.g., in the case of
Isaiah's prophecy) and, in the Christian context, how God has
acted in Christ.

Gustafson returns to the viewpoint we are seeking to make
clear when he says:

In the ethics of discipleship to Jesus Christ . . . there is a weight of
obligation to be willing to suffer and to die for the sake of the needs of
the neighbor, or for the sake of the cause of witnessing to the requirements of peace, justice, and love in the world. There is a heavy pull toward the pacifist position, not only because of the primacy of love, but
also because of many sayings, actions, and implications from varieties of
literature in the New Testament.[19]

"To suffer and die for the sake of the needs of the neighbor"
has a distinct Markan stamp on it, and we are prepared to concur
in Gustafson's evaluation of the New Testament witness, if he does
not mean that one must also be prepared to kill for the sake of
peace, justice, and love in the world. Since he quotes in this same
article, without rebuttal, the pungent student axiom that "killing for the sake of peace is like fornicating for the sake of
virginity," one may be justified in assuming that Gustafson
(without H. Richard Niebuhr's uncertainty on the point) places
Jesus and the New Testament under the first type, Christ against
culture.[20] This does not mean that Gustafson, against both H.
Richard and Reinhold Niebuhr, advocates a pacifist or nonviolent ethic for contemporary Christianity. It does clarify the
fact that neither the Gospels nor the early church can be brought
under the typology finally espoused in the Niebuhrian ethic. When
S. G. F. Brandon sets about his task of ridding the Gospels of
the portrait of the pacific Christ, he is at least to be commended
for discerning what is obvious in what the evangelists say. His

extensive revisionist approach is necessitated by the fact that he has gotten Mark's message.

This brings us to a second objection to H. Richard Niebuhr's typology. By his definition of culture, the specific problem of violence within culture is obscured, and, in a sense, made palatable. *Christ and Culture* reveals two presuppositions on culture that do not receive validation: the autonomy of culture (i.e., its independence of Christ) and its monolithic character.[21] Both of these presuppositions imply that culture has a totalitarian character permitting no selectivity, no discrimination. This is an unwarranted implication with respect to what culture is and what the most radical of Christians have represented in their cultural attitudes.

Niebuhr selects the First Letter of John as "the least ambiguous presentation of this point of view" (i.e., Christ against culture).[22] His treatment of "the world" as it appears in this epistle is a good case in point.[23] It can be said with certainty that 1 John does not use "the world" for what is meant by "culture." "The world" in the Johannine literature is a special term expressing the moral dualism on which Johannine theology is predicated. "World" in 1 John is not the *kosmos* as a neutral entity, but the *kosmos* in so far as it expresses the working of evil in a coherent and structured way. Thus the rejection or judgment of the world in 1 John is not an example of cultural rejection in some total sense but of that in the world that, specifically, is evil. If culture as "civilization" comprises among other things language, 1 John would be expected to deliver some pronouncements against language (especially Greek as the language of culture).[24] Yet Greek is found a convenient and acceptable vehicle for its message. Poetry as an art form certainly underlies 1 John 2:12–14, but the author has no scruples against so expressing himself and thus evidences a procultural viewpoint. Typologies of the kind employed by Niebuhr in *Christ and Culture* cannot, of necessity, take into account all the exceptions and variant shades of meaning within each type. In this case, however, the

116 JESUS AND THE POLITICS OF VIOLENCE

exceptions are serious enough to show that the category Christ against culture is inadmissible as a description of the social outlook of the early Christians. Niebuhr's conclusion that Christ against culture is an impossible stance, furthermore, is already contained in the presuppositions that underlie his definition of culture.

In dealing with 1 John, Niebuhr treats "the world" as a pseudonym for "culture" and the world as "heir of Cain."[25] In the literature of the Johannine epistles, this reference to Cain is striking in that it is the only explicit Old Testament allusion contained in these epistles. The reference is found in 1 John 3:12, and it gives specific content to what the writer of 1 John means by "the world." In the context of 1 John 3:12 the author is in the middle of a section on love, treating his theme with his characteristic antithetical style (i.e., righteousness, love, belief, and their opposites). Cain enters as the antithesis of love, an archetype of hatred issuing in personal violence: he "slew" (the Greek verb *sphazein* has a crude and bloody implication) his brother. This reference pointedly indicates what 1 John means by "the world."

When established states write and teach their history, they censor from it moral disapproval of the violence that was involved. Guilt and disapproval are transferred to the aboriginal people or the successive enemies of the state whose conquest has been necessary for the manifest destiny of the nation's power. So the writing of history in the various national communities, and even in the sectional subcommunities, consists largely in a chronicle of the glorious violence by which the frontier was expanded, dissident elements crushed, and foreign foes compelled to surrender. The "bad history" that Gen. Maxwell Taylor bemoaned as a consequence of the publication of the Pentagon Papers on the Vietnam war is that in which the glory of national violence is sullied by criticism or accused of dishonesty.[26]

In recent times, Jacques Ellul was constrained to emphasize the intimate kinship between government and violence because unrealistic political thinking, based on nationalistic rather than humanistic or Christian principles, pictures government and the order it imposes as essentially nonviolent. Correctively, Ellul is led to define government and its works with a vigorous but informed realism. "Every state," Ellul writes, "is founded on violence and cannot maintain itself save by and through violence."[27]

It is this kind of essential (i.e., dealing with the essence of things) thinking that marks the writer of 1 John. This is the understanding of human institutions that constitutes Christian belief as a radical and revolutionary force in a continuous, nonviolent sense. When Christ was condemned by the state to die with criminals, it profoundly shaped the cultural outlook by which government was comprehended in the Christian tradition. That outlook is implicit in the *theologia crucis*. Rome's pacification of its eastern frontier meant one thing to the Roman senate. It meant something else to Christians out on the boundary where the sentence of death had fallen upon their lord.

For western Christians habituated to a cultural optimism about the nature and possibilities of governmental power, it seems not only erroneous but positively evil to comprehend government and law *sub specie violentiae*. In the fall of 1970, however, not long before his indictment for sheltering Daniel Berrigan when Berrigan was a fugitive from the FBI for destroying Selective Service files in Catonsville, Maryland, William Stringfellow wrote of the state of American life in these terms:

In this tentative, uneasy perception, I believe, a host of citizens, otherwise subdued, grasp the desperate issue that is taking place in America now: the power of death incarnate in the State violating, enslaving, perverting, imprisoning, destroying human life in society. To fail or refuse to act against that power amounts to an abdication of one's humanness, a renunciation of the lives of other human beings, a very ignominious idolatry of death. In the face of that power the only way to act—no matter how the State judges or what the State does—is to live in the authority over death that the resurrection is.[28]

One recognizes, of course, that this radical view of the state (as opposed, for example, to that in Romans 13) is not valid at all times and in all circumstances. When, however, Niebuhr's use of culture is designed to represent its beneficial possibilities under the transformation of Christ, the demonic capability of culture is so camouflaged that the realism one normally associates with the name Niebuhr succumbs to false ideas of progress.

The third objection to the solution proposed by both H. Richard and Reinhold Niebuhr to the issue of violence is a pragmatic one, namely, that the strategy of transforming the institution of war (certainly to be ranked among the major instruments of civilization), either in terms of its elimination or its "Christianization," has been so fully unsuccessful as to show that the theory itself, not just its application, is untenable. While Reinhold Niebuhr disliked the term "just war," because it failed to express clearly the evil that war is and tended toward self-righteousness, his well-known essay, "Why the Christian Church Is Not Pacifist," provided the ideological catalyst by which the Christian majority put aside the antimilitary ideals of the 1930s and girded itself for the grim tasks of 1941–45.[29] When Paul Ramsey openly identifies with the just war tradition, it is an explicit acknowledgement of what is implicit in the theology of the Niebuhrs. To deal with the consequences of the theory of just war in the history of the Christian majority, three lines of inquiry are suggested: the issue of selective objection; World War II as the cause of World War III; and the legitimacy of revolutionary violence.

1. SELECTIVE CONSCIENTIOUS OBJECTION. It is wholly consistent with the Christian theory of just war (taken over from Cicero) and with Reinhold Niebuhr's "lesser of two evils" principle that some wars are unjust or that the position of both antagonists in a given conflict cannot be equally just. Presumably, Christians who happen to be on the wrong side should not lend support to their government in an aggression against an adversary trying to defend himself.

Persistent political efforts by the Mennonites, Friends, Brethren, and other minority sects (about whom the Niebuhrs have few kind remarks) yielded legislative recognition for the right of religious objection to all wars. The entire history of the just war tradition, however, has yielded no legislative recognition by which those who judged a specific war to be unjust might act upon their moral conviction without breaking the law. In 1961, Paul Ramsey advocated "discretionary armed service," and in January 1971, Representative Edward Koch introduced in the House of Representatives a bill (H.R. 832) designed to allow conscientious opposition to service in a particular war.[30] One views these efforts with hope rather than disdain, but the long history (since Constantine) of the complete absence of any Christian strategy for dealing with "unjust" wars encourages the impression that from the beginning of the just war theory its major intent was to remove the moral impediments hampering Christian participation in war as an "extension of government."

The war in Vietnam has brought this issue into painful prominence. It is an enduring monument to the integrity of Reinhold Niebuhr (as over against many of his protégés) that from at least 1966 he spoke against the American policy in Southeast Asia. By 1969, the Catholic bishops of the United States, the National and World Council of Churches, and virtually all the major denominational bodies in the United States had urged the enactment of laws allowing selective objection. In 1971, the Synagogue Council of America, the central coordinating agency for American Jewry, also adopted a major policy statement supporting this position.

The legislative feasability of selective objection had, however, been brought under consideration by the Marshall Commission in 1967, and it had formulated a somewhat official governmental response on the subject. Chaired by Burke Marshall, former assistant attorney general, the commission presented its study of the Selective Service System to President Johnson in

February 1967. Five reasons were given for refusing the right of what the commission, in a clever piece of phrase-making, called "selective pacifism."[31] The first four of these reasons may be summarized as follows:

1. Only total objection to all killing in war can be legally administered, because selective pacifism would introduce situational moral judgments and cause the government to invade the domain of differing denominational definitions of just and unjust wars.

2. Selective pacifism would be "a political question of support or nonsupport of a war and cannot be judged in terms of special moral imperatives."

3. Selective pacifism would invite a selective disobedience (as in the case of a particular tax) to other laws as well.

4. Selective pacifism would render impossible noncombatant military service (such as the medics), because such objectors would not consent to be agents in a war that they had already judged to be unjust.

One reluctantly abstains from commenting on the surprising logic of these opinions in order to devote more specific attention to the fifth and final reason adduced by the commission against selective objection. It is a capstone for the other arguments:

Finally, the majority felt that a legal recognition of selective pacifism could be disruptive to the morale and effectiveness of the armed forces. A determination of the justness or unjustness of any war could only be made within the context of that war itself. Forcing upon the individual the necessity of making that decision—which would be the practical effect of taking away the government's obligation of making it for him— could put a burden heretofore unknown on the man in uniform and even on the brink of combat, with results that could well be disastrous to him, to his unit and to the entire military tradition. No such problem arises for the conscientious objector in uniform, who bases his moral stand on killing in all forms, simply because he is never trained for nor assigned to combat duty.[32]

Apparently the commission remained unmoved by recent Christian emphasis on contextual ethics, for one can scarcely find a statement more clearly devoted to the prescriptive, fundamentalist type of moral decision. The commission states that it is the government's obligation to decide for the individual whether the war is just. This one opinion renders nonexistent the idea of just or unjust warfare, since a government would never engage in a war and simultaneously admit it to be unjust. Perhaps the most singular feature of the statement, however, is the judgment that selective objection would be a disaster to the whole military tradition. That may indeed be the reason behind all reasons why no government has ever enacted legislation giving serious embodiment to the theory of just war as it bears concretely on the right of conscience among the men required to bear the arms.

The position of the Marshall Commission on selective objection was reinforced by the Supreme Court on 8 March 1971, in the decisions on Gillette v. United States and Negre v. Larsen. In these judgments the court refused to broaden the law on conscientious objection to cover objection to service in the Vietnam war specifically. These cases were not explicit judgments on the moral rectitude of selective objection, but were opinions affirming that when the Congress ruled out selective objection, while allowing for conscientious objection to all wars, it did not act in violation of the First Amendment. The appellants argued that Congress had favored the historic "peace churches" (Friends, Mennonites, Brethren, etc.) but had discriminated against the major religious bodies such as the Catholic church, whose moral teaching supported selective objection. Louis Negre, a Catholic, had carefully studied Aquinas and other advocates of the just war theory.

The court's decision "dwelt at length on the Government's assertions that its military capacity might be paralyzed if selective conscientious objection were recognized as a constitutional right."[33] Curtis Tarr, the director of Selective Service, was reported to be relieved by the decision of the court "because he believed the draft system could not operate if selective conscientious objection were authorized."[34] If in a country like the United States, which considers itself quite advanced in human rights and civil liberties, this is what legislative and governmental opinion on the theory of just war has come to, as concretely expressed in selective objection, it is not intemperate to judge that the impact of the theory of just war as a "transformer" of the institution of war has been nil.

2. WORLD WAR II AS THE CAUSE OF WORLD WAR III.   It is the constant dream of men in all nations and a necessary part of the political speechmaking in which national leaders engage that war is to be phased out of human experience. Religious men are particularly prone to share this dream. Herein we meet a feature of the perennial dialectic of war, namely, that its cruelty for the time is tolerable because its extinction will soon be accomplished.

The same logic attends the work of revolutionary movements. That is, the acts of terror, assassination, political imprisonment, and purge by death committed against representatives of the old regime are temporary necessities that can be eliminated as soon as the injustices of the counterrevolutionaries are eliminated. As soon as reactionary attitudes are corrected violence will depart, because justice, which is the foundation of peace, will have been established.

These ideas have amazing persistence. They bring us again into the Orwellian world where the great fighters are in fact the great peacemakers, where, indeed, warmaking is peacemaking. Against this view, we propose that violence fosters violence, war fosters war, and that the history of Christian endorsement of war exhibits neither the amelioration of war nor the lessening of its violence, but its intensification. At the same moment the integrity of religious belief is impoverished. In Niebuhrian terms, what ensues is not the transformation of culture but the transformation of Christ.

World War II laid the foundations for World War III just as World War I laid the foundations for World War II. German military science pioneered many devastating improvements both in equipment and tactics by which the power to strike, kill, and overcome could be increased. Great new devices of propaganda were brought into play to weld the people into an efficient fighting unit. The allied powers adopted and advanced the German techniques. After the war German missile experts transferred their scientific genius to the allied victors, east and west, where they continued to bring the mechanics of war to fuller perfection. With saturation bombing, gigantic incendiary raids, and guided missiles, destruction and death were carried to the remotest civilian communities. By the time the allied policy of unconditional surrender was firmly established and Hiroshima and Nagasaki were atom-bombed in 1945, it is possible that some Christian moralists far removed from the decision-making processes of government had begun to question whether the limits of just war had been transgressed.[35]

Germany was cut in two. No treaty for the settlement of the German question was ever written, because the policy of Communist containment, quiescent during the war, broke out again very quickly when combat ceased. Germany divided remains a running sore of actual and potential violence in the middle of Europe, as East Germany was incorporated into the defense perimeter of the Soviet Union just as West Germany had been incorporated into the defense perimeter of the United States. Marxism, faltering seriously prior to World War II, received massive allied aid and consolidated its position despite the great cost the war demanded in the suffering of the Russian people. Eastern Europe came under Marxist control.

The Jews were not saved by the war. The most massive crimes against the Jewish people were carried out under the cover of darkness imposed by the war itself. The Wannsee Conference, proposing its "final solution to the Jewish problem," did not take place until 1942. Late in the war Jewish refugees seeking haven in the United States were cruelly turned away from American shores and sent back to whatever destiny might await them in the Europe from which they had already fled.[36] America and Britain felt great guilt over the fate of the Jews and sought a solution by transferring the problem to the Middle East where, subsequently, violence has been chronic and escalating.

The war stopped Hitler, but not Hitlerism. All across the globe American power was polarized with the Marxism that the war had helped to stabilize. The prodigal use of human and material resources required by the war was not redirected toward the alleviation of poverty. Conditions of want, already widespread in the world and aggravated by the economics of war, further encouraged the growth of Marxist ideology. The test of American alliance-making was not whether a government was democratic, upheld constitutional authority, and defended civil liberty, but whether it was anti-Communist. Thus General Ky of South Vietnam, who expressed open admiration for Hitler, became, along with other officers who were trained by and fought with the French in Indochina against the nationalist (and Communist) Viet Minh, a trusted figure of American policy in Southeast Asia. Saigon practiced so wantonly the politics of political imprisonment, news censorship, and forced population relocation under threat of death, that what was done in the name of freedom could not be distinguished from the worst that could be feared from totalitarianism. Chiang Kai-Shek came under extraordinary American patronage in a vain and provocative effort to treat mainland China as nonexistent, despite his ruthless and bloody repression of indigenous Formosans and practice of police state politics. The Ping Pong diplomacy of 1971 offered prospects of a change in the Far East containment doctrine, though the final toll of violence wrought by the politics of counterrevolution in Greece, Spain, Indonesia, Latin America, and Africa has yet to be measured.

Developments within the United States during World War II

give the explosive conditions of the postwar world an understandable coherence. When Eisenhower deplored the influence of the
military-industrial complex over all of American culture in his
retirement speech of 18 January 1961, it must have been obvious except to the most unthinking that he was himself both
the product and the promoter of that which he deplored. War and
violence are intimately related to economic factors. America's
struggle with domestic economic stagnation in the 1930s did not
come to completion before the intervention of World War II. The
WPA yielded to the WPB.[37] The control of the military, industrial, and political elite whose management was necessary to make
World War II and the ideology that justifies endless, ever-
mounting expenditures for military power have retained continuous dominance since 1945. The Pentagon behemoth, with its
vast network of connections in the political and industrial community, bestows its huge rewards on those sectors of the economy
whose aggrandizement effects the peculiar kind of national socialism that can erupt both at home and abroad in repressive violence. Russia and other nations have their own counterparts to
American Pentagonism. The political weight of the military di-
rectorates is such that Britain, for example, despite vigorous disapproval by the Commonwealth states and the United Nations,
proceeds with the sale of arms to South Africa, strengthening that
government against its black majority. America provides some re-
lief money for India's back-breaking effort to cope with refugees
flooding in from East Pakistan at the same time that American-
made arms make possible ruthless devastation of the land and its
people. Simultaneously, a black revolutionary in California, An-
gela Davis, is brought to trial for the alleged crime of providing
guns employed in acts of violence.

    Rational Christians disavow, of course, the evil consequences
of World War II and the contribution they make to World
War III. Yet this disavowal has not yet yielded any general dis-
enchantment among the Christian majority with the rationale by

which churchly support for previous wars has been guaranteed. Rule books on how nuclear war or counterinsurgency war can be waged without going against the guidelines of Augustine or Aquinas have already been drawn up at the same time that solemn lamentations are voiced over our march toward extinction. As the history of civilization is drawn out, the limits of destructive capacity relentlessly expand. After each orgy of civil or international violence subsides, new vows of "Never again!" are sworn by all participants while preparations for the next round continue as before. The aggregate annual arms expenditures of the nations now exceed two hundred billion dollars, with more to come. The dreamers naïvely assure us that the violence of war is getting so massive that men will turn from it "of necessity." Thus the doomsday weapons that have no brains are pictured as the deliverance of the men who make them, a logic very persuasive among those who believe in peace through violence.

Let us assume that the drift toward World War III continues and that we do fight this war with nuclear weapons. Let us further assume, depending on the "credibility of our defenses" (i.e., how much more power is to be bequeathed to the Pentagon), that a half or three-fourths or even more of our people can survive "a general nuclear exchange," as Herman Kahn and other experts predict. What change of conditions conducive to peace would this disaster accomplish? Does not history show that human thinking would continue as before to explain that the war was caused by disarmament, by the disdain of the political and military expertise that alone is competent to make the arrangements necessary for peace, that war and violence are biologically rooted and hence inevitable, or, most exasperating of all, that Jesus predicted wars would come and so it is useless to try to stop them? It must be considered, on the contrary, that the escalating levels of violence that war requires are contributing to the depletion of those resources, human and material, moral and economic, that are necessary for the elimination of violence.

Poverty causes violence. As Russia and the United States vie for supremacy in weapons (balance of power, translated, always means "balance in our favor"), the billions of dollars necessary for world development are spent on arms and arms development to the special advantage of selected segments of the respective domestic economies. The deprived poor are radicalized by want. The United States and the Soviet Union are converted to programs of counterrevolutionary violence in their separate spheres of influence, and this tendency would not be halted but encouraged by the depleting effects of World War III. The technology of war is cauterizing the human conscience. The transfer of the battle scene to the living room by instant communications does not sensitize and humanize the viewers mechanically any more than combat humanizes the combatants. Aerial attack is less personal and more inhumane—if such a comparison has any meaning—than ground fighting. Yet, just as killing with a gun seems "cleaner" than killing with a hatchet, the impersonalization of rocket and missile warfare increases the cruelty and volume of destruction while persuading the destroyer that he is exhibiting moral progress.

Many or most of these deplorable developments arose during World War II. They drag the world, willingly or not, toward increasing violence and the outbreak of World War III.

3. THE LEGITIMACY OF REVOLUTIONARY VIOLENCE. We have earlier referred to "Christians for violence" in the context of social change and the plight of the colonized people of the world. Out of intimate acquaintance with the social and economic conditions that prevail in the poorer nations, not a few missionaries like Richard Shaull and Thomas Melville in the locale of their ministries in Latin America have asserted with regret that the hope of democratic change without resort to violence is an impossible dream. The year before his death as a guerrilla fighter with the Colombian Army of National Liberation in February 1966, the Reverend Camilo Torres had written:

But violence is not excluded from the Christian ethic, because if Christianity is concerned with eliminating the serious evils which we suffer and saving us from the continuous violence in which we live without possible solution, the ethic is to be violence once and for all in order to destroy the violence which the economic minorities exercise against the people.[38]

These sentiments were echoed in 1970 in *Violence in Southern Africa, A Christian Assessment,* issued by a committee of the Department of International Affairs of the British Council of Churches and the Conference of British Missionary Societies. Churchmen of the United Kingdom were jolted by the content of this report, because it gave clear sanction to the use of violence as a last resort in efforts to remove the inequities of white supremacy in southern Africa. Five territories were placed under review in this study: South Africa, South-West Africa, Rhodesia, Angola, and Mozambique. In these regions, four million whites rule over thirty-one million blacks, controlling the processes of law and government so totally that many African Christians have concluded that "unconstitutional action is the only course left open."[39]

Just as in America black leadership after 1968 began to look back upon the tactics of Martin Luther King as a past era, the aspirations of African blacks broke over the bounds of patience counseled by the nonviolence of leaders like Albert Luthuli.[40] The report to the British Council of Churches therefore concludes:

The action of those in rebellion, as of those at war, must be subject to moral judgment, both as to means and as to objects. Those who are themselves in comfort and security cannot urge armed rebellion on others who would thereby face death or life imprisonment. Nor can they preach patient endurance of a suffering they do not have to bear. *But there can be a just rebellion as well as a just war and we cannot sincerely withhold support from those who have decided to face the certain suffering involved in such liberation.*[41]

As a matter of historical interest, the theory of just war formalized in Augustine and Ambrose stipulated, among other things, that to be just a war should be declared by a legitimate authority.[42] This aspect of the Augustinian idea was obviously oriented toward the rejection of revolutionary violence within the Roman empire. Because revolutionary war would be declared by an authority that the state had not legitimated, it could not *ipso facto* be just. Since, however, the Augustinian guidelines in both Catholicism and Protestantism have been subject to various official emendations, there is no compelling reason why Christians today should not lay down rules for a just rebellion that is parallel to just war. Certainly the breach of these rules in the one case would not be more frequent than it was in the other.

In September 1970, the Executive Committee of the World Council of Churches allocated grants from its Special Fund to Combat Racism to nineteen organizations in Europe, Asia, Latin America, and Africa that are engaged in various efforts to overcome ethnic injustice, mainly that arising from white supremacy. It was specified that these grants were not for the purchase of arms nor for direct support of military activities, but should be used for purposes consistent with the aims and character of the World Council. Despite these precautions, reaction against the grants has been quite pronounced, especially among churches of white membership in southern Africa. *Violence in Southern Africa* also failed to gain an endorsement vote when the British Council met in November 1970 at Swansea, Wales. The Christian majority, though not endorsing pacifism itself, seems determined to apply the criterion of nonviolence to all the liberation movements. This can only result in the impression that the white Christians impose a standard of morality upon blacks (or upon other nonwhite people) that they themselves have not attained.

The Christian church in America was split down the middle on the Vietnam war. Those who seriously attempted to apply the criteria of just war to the Vietnam conflict were able to mount significant if not decisive churchly opposition to the government's policy.[43] This opposition gives rise to the following question: If the arguments against the justice of the Vietnam war were valid, did that not oblige Christian advocates of just war to take up arms against their own American government in support of the National Liberation Front of South Vietnam? To ask the question is to answer it.

We conclude, therefore, that the "lawful violence" that has been presupposed in the Christian majority from the time of Constantine fails, on pragmatic grounds, to establish its validity. It has proven to be a means not of Christianizing war but of militarizing Christianity. If there is a just war, there must also be a just revolution. Faced with that possibility, however, the Christian majority assumes the pacifist position that violence is wrong. Thus the church evidences an almost fatalistic tendency to identify with counterrevolution. Its outreach to the nonwhite majority of the world's people faces the insuperable barrier of inviting that majority to embrace a faith only guaranteeing to it the perpetuation of white favoritism.

The Imitation of Christ

In previous chapters an effort has been made in accord with acceptable critical guidelines to discover the attitude toward violence that the portrait of Jesus in the Gospels has recorded. This investigation rests in part on a classical Christian assumption that Christ constitutes a model that is normative for Christian behavior. This assumption is illustrated in the fact that the word "Christian," when applied to moral attitudes or behavior, is used most frequently in the sense of "Christlike." There are, to be sure, other, more sophisticated ethical uses of the term "Christian" that cannot be disregarded, but we refer here to everyday, conversational, rather than to academic, language.

Objections to the effort to treat Christ as an ethical model are numerous and weighty. Since Albert Schweitzer, for example, the element of eschatology has caused serious difficulty in knowing what kind of apocalyptic presuppositions underlay the teaching of Jesus. Schweitzer's analysis of Jesus' ethic has not been unchallenged. Bultmann, not famous for critical inhibitions, wrote of it:

> The investigation has shown that both the eschatological and the ethical teaching of Jesus belong equally to the oldest stratum of the tradition, so that one can hardly call either one of them secondary. Nor can we view the ethical precepts of Jesus as "interim-ethic" . . . for his demands have an absolute character, and are by no means influenced in their formulation by the thought that the end of the world is near at hand. Consequently, both sides of the message, the eschatological and the ethical, must be conceived as belonging together.[44]

If, however, the eschatological as well as the ethical receive in Bultmann's existential interpretation what may be called a symbolical rather than a historical treatment, the place of Jesus as model for the ethical life is no less problematical in Bultmann than in Schweitzer. It is certain that in modern Christianity the eschatological ideas of the early church receive only token treatment. So it is awkward, to say the least, to take the moral precept of Jesus seriously without being able to determine or accept the historical or cosmological presuppositions in which it was initially expressed.

We cannot, furthermore, form a consistent picture of what Jesus did or said about numerous moral concerns that weigh upon the contemporary conscience. How is the model of Jesus to be transferred to the critical dilemmas of unemployment, abortion, the rights of women, cybernation, drugs, and environmental control—to name only a few. When we are driven in such matters to deduce from general ethical premises such as love, faithfulness, and humility what the model of Jesus would look like in the contemporary moral struggle, we only discover how strongly and sincerely men can differ when they proceed from the abstract guideline to the concrete situation. Even when Christians have ascribed to Jesus the place of preeminent example in the making of moral judgments, their conclusions on contemporary problems have been widely divergent. Information as to the physiological or psychological consequences of this or that form of conduct is often conflicting and usually incomplete, so that moral judgments not only suffer emendation as information is altered, but may even be diametrically reversed. What place, moreover, in a spectrum of authority is to be assigned to Old Testament ethics, the ethics of Paul, of James, and so on? H. Richard Niebuhr and others have correctly emphasized that the church itself, its creeds and councils, have had a potent effect on the moral understanding of Christianity.

The older notion of Protestantism that the Scripture "judges" the church is compromised by the fact that the churchly situation seriously affected both the form and the content of the Scripture. "Canon" is itself a churchly creation. This basic finding of the form critical method is also applicable to the portrait of Christ that the Gospels yield. There is no unmediated line of contact with Jesus. Decisive moral insights have been brought to Christianity by emphasis upon the inner light or the Spirit, as emphasized among the Friends, for example, but, again, the precise bearing of this on Jesus as model is variously construed.

None of these difficulties in moving from the portrait of Jesus to the contemporary situation can be lightly treated. Nor can they be allowed to have the final word.

In discussing H. Richard Niebuhr's use of the Bible in Christian ethics, Gustafson defines biblicism as: "that in which the Bible becomes too exclusively the source of knowledge for man's ethical responsibility, and in which men feel prone to find the biblical theological foundations for every serious moral act or thought."[45] The fulcrum of this description is the adverbial clause "too exclusively," for that is the problem that the definition is seeking to clarify. "Exclusively" is, by itself, a categorical expression. "Too" is added in order to moderate the effect of "exclusively" without abandoning its categorical aspect. What is actually at stake is the question of continuity with Christian origins. We have previously dealt with this in the discussion of H. Richard Niebuhr's *Christ and Culture*. It is the question of permanence and change, of norms and situations.

When H. Richard Niebuhr reacts against Bultmann and Barth for describing biblical ethics in terms of obedience rather than response, it is likely that the critical point of difference is the question of whether the Bible (or Christ and the Gospels within the Bible) constitutes a proper basis for building Christian moral thought.[46] Bultmann's "radical obedience," like his existential interpretation, is, in fact, a response kind of understanding in that Bultmann works almost exclusively from the faith/works dialectic of Paul, with its antilegal bias. Bultmann placed radical obedience in opposition to formal obedience along lines that anticipated the prescriptive versus situational ethics debate long before it became fashionable. It was his radical preoccupation with the kerygma (God's action in the Gospel, to put it in Niebuhr's categories) and his (Pauline) apprehension about human achievement on the basis of the "law" that prompted Bultmann to assign ethics a place of obscurity in Christian theology. After all, it is not just the ceremonial or ritual aspects of the law that are attacked by Paul's polemic against "works of the law," but the moral aspects as well.[47] This drove Bultmann and his followers to maintain a greater distance from social ethics and political engagement than Barth and the Barthians, a cleavage that echoes in its own way Luther and Calvin respectively.

It may be rightly questioned, therefore, whether H. Richard Niebuhr, in drawing such a contrast between the ethic of deon-

tology (i.e., obligation or obedience to a biblical precedent) and
that of responsibility, has done more than reformulate in an interesting way the place that the paradigm of Christ occupies in the
Christian understanding of ethics. This is particularly the case if
Christ as model is conceived as gift, the *datum*, or the action of
God to which man in faith responds. This understanding of New
Testament ethics, furthermore, should not be set apart by contrast from what is found in the Old Testament, since the Exodus
is the redemptive action on which the ethos of the community's
life is constructed. Just so, the first word of the decalogue is not
a statement of obligation, but of divine action: "I am the Lord
your God, who brought you out of the land of Egypt, out of the
house of bondage" (Exod. 20:2).

Christianity derives its historical consciousness from what
happened in the first century, understood in faith as the fulfillment of the messianic hope. The tradition of Jesus is the normative factor that allows us to speak of the Christian ethic. This
does not mean, to use an example, that biblical studies must be
the prima donna in the theological tradition. There is a difference
between formal primacy and real primacy. Historical or pastoral
theology or social ethics may embrace more of the reality of the
tradition of Jesus than courses in the Greek exegesis of Mark. At
the same time, we cannot avoid asking what claim this or that
ethical development can make to the designation "Christian." By
the same token that our hackles rise at phrases like *deutsche
Christen* or "for Christians only," because we resent the meaning
that is attached to "Christian" in these phrases, the determination
of the moral content of Christianity must be undertaken in a
manner that allows us to retain Christianity's historical identity.
If this violates H. Richard Niebuhr's axiom that the Bible cannot
be set in a "chain of command" or a rank of authority that varies
in precedence from contemporary philosophy or councils of the
church or the movement of the Spirit or the conscientious intui-
tion of devout men, then it is a violation that we will have to

risk. Correspondingly, Gustafson's (condescending?) reference to those who seek a model to which they can conform their action (similarly, "if one must have an ideal or example") invites the response that there is in the final analysis no ethical style that operates without models both dominant and subdominant, just as there is no person who comes to any context of decision exempt from the preformative experiences, conscious or otherwise, to which he has been subject.[48] In this matter, what is to be feared is not the person who tries to define his model, but the one who claims he has none.

The quest for freedom is unending and indispensable. Freedom, however, is threatened not merely by tradition but also by discontinuity. One readily agrees that the imitation of Christ in the history of Christian thought has been as much abused by an oppressive legalism as by a naïve sentimentality. Nevertheless, the Christ of the machine gun, whatever scenario (right or left) is set for the model, evokes a clash of images that for reasons elaborated in this book stands solidly against the earliest impression Christ made on men and substantially jeopardizes the continuity with its origins that Christian confession affirms.

The rise of historical criticism has made it clear that the Jesus of history and the Christ of faith are set forth in the New Testament as one, composite figure. The possibility always exists that definitive historical evidence might be produced to show that Jesus was, historically speaking, radically different from the portraits that faith has made of him: that he was a megalomaniac, a guerrilla fighter, a homosexual with compensatory sublimations, a student of Socrates, a man from Mars, or a figment of the phallic mushroom imagination. All of these suggestions, and more, have been made, laying claim to historical finality. Many would feel in the face of such a "scientific discovery" that the image of Jesus that is projected across the screen of the Gospels would no longer hold any interest for men.

That conclusion does not necessarily follow.

It is already evident to historical awareness that Christ as model stands on the boundary between history and faith, because "model" stands apart (despite continuity) from that which it represents. Thus the example of Christ presented in the Gospel tradition would be judged as to its credibility, its value, and its usefulness from considerations that are independent of what we refer to as the historical Jesus. If, furthermore, it could be shown that no such model man as the Gospels exhibit actually existed, then it would be forthwith necessary for the moral sanity of the world to create one.

Critical historical inquiry in the Gospels is an enterprise of human intelligence that has gone on from the beginning of Christianity. In its complexity and magnitude there is no branch of scientific research to surpass it. Despite the many nonhistorical elements that the record of Jesus has been shown to contain, they do not render the model substantially or significantly unsupportable. The quest of the historical Jesus will not and should not be repudiated, but after centuries of endlessly novel proposals from this quarter and that, the Christian faith acquires an understandable reluctance to dance for every new piper.

Aggressive Man/Nonviolent Man

It is altogether obvious that the human model may be formed out of materials that have nothing to do with Christ or any religious tradition. Indeed, in a nonreligious epoch, biblical patterns of thought would appear to be the exception. In recent years the role of violence in the animal kingdom has been made the subject of investigation by Robert Ardrey, Konrad Lorenz, and others.[49] The model that emerges from these studies is the Man of Aggression.

Ardrey attempted to show in *African Genesis* that the primitive tools found at Olduvai Gorge in Tanganyika belonged to an ape (not man) who was vegetarian and pacifist. This ape was overwhelmed by an ape that killed. From the latter descended man, so that the archetypal man is a predator "whose natural instinct is to kill with a weapon." The development and use of weapons, therefore, is the distinguishing feature of human evolution and culture.

In *The Territorial Imperative,* Ardrey drew upon John Calhoun's experiments with rats at the National Institute of Mental Health and observations of the langur monkeys in Ceylon and India by Phyllis Dolhinov, Suzanne Ripley, and Yukimaru Sugiyama to demonstrate that violence increases as room or natural spacing in the environment is diminished. An instinctive order exists in nature, based not only on the respective roles of male and female but also on the capacities of power and dominance that mark the organizational structure of the species. Animals and men reject anonymity, boredom, and anxiety. They seek identity, stimulation, and security. When the territory is penetrated by strangers, the violence already invited by boredom is triggered in quest of security. Thus xenophobia is a major catalyst of violence, and violence, like pornography, is pursued for excitement and fun.

Ardrey completes the picture of the Man of Aggression by arguing in *The Social Contract* that Rousseau insincerely fostered the utopian dream of equality and was ignorant of the observations reported later by Darwin. There is no equality among men or animals. Egalitarian social ideals that inspire the liberation movements contradict the model of dominance and the rule of violence that we learn from zoology. As the laws of spacing are violated in the human habitat, we can look for the continued increase of violence until the instinct for order prevails over the danger of anarchy. While the level of violence is dangerously high, our major threat is domestic violence, because war between

nations will gradually decline since it is either catastrophic (nuclear) or inconclusive (Vietnam, the Middle East).

There has been no dearth of writers to find fault with Ardrey's
model of man. Thomas Merton called it "pseudo-science."[50] Following Ashley-Montagu, Nieburg objected to the notion of "innate
depravity" (i.e., violence as an ancestral trait) because it con-
fuses what is inherited with what is acquired and tends to justify,
sanction, or even idealize violence.[51] Nieburg emphasizes the
acquisition of new and unprecedented characteristics in anmial
behavior. Hannah Arendt (criticizing Lorenz's biological theories
of aggression) objects to the "misleading transposition of physical
terms such as 'energy' and 'force' to biological and zoological
data."[52] She also objects to Lorenz's dependence on an outmoded
anthropology that treats man as the *animal rationale,* like other
beasts except in the additional attribute of reason.

Biblical thought is not naïvely cut off from the human model
proposed in zoological research. Ardrey exploits the Cain-Abel
typology for its appropriate illustration of the decisive, primordial
struggle.[53] Paul, in the famous typology of Romans 3:10–18, is
fully appraised of the nature of human aggression and, drawing
upon various psalms, declaims in summary: "None is righteous,
no, not one; . . . Their feet are swift to shed blood, in their paths
are ruin and misery, and the way of peace they do not know."

One is struck with the extent to which aggressiveness and
violence become the new original sin in social anthropology.[54]
What kind of order can be expected to emerge from the model
of aggressive man except the one we already have? Rousseau may
have fostered mistaken ideas about human equality, but, as
Nieburg (against Ardrey) warns, to give ideological sanction to
oligarchical concepts of civic life confirms the presuppositions of
the class struggle and multiplies the likelihood of violent unrest.

It is certainly optimistic to assume that war will phase out of
history because it is becoming either catastrophic or inconclusive.
All wars are catastrophic, and it is not just recent ones that are

to be defined as inconclusive—if, indeed, they deserve that description. The history of modern Israel, spelled out in bloody conflict with Egypt, cannot be called, to this date, "inconclusive," for even the Egyptians have been compelled to acknowledge the enormous gains that Israel has amassed. Nor does one get the impression that either Hanoi or the NLF in South Vietnam regards the Vietnam war as inconclusive, though Washington would have doubtless been happy by the end of 1971 to get by with that description of it. A random sampling of political and military conduct since 1940 does not encourage the notion that leaders of nations or the people they represent are governed by rational calculations as to the costs and consequences of belligerency. We must add to this that as nuclear weapons proliferate, the opportunity of accidents and maverick, irrational outbursts increases.

These objections to the idea of aggressive man are not introduced, however, for the purpose of showing that the model of social organization based on human aggression is not scientifically acceptable. Let us assume for the moment that the biological studies of Ardrey and others are descriptively correct and that the ethical and political deductions drawn from them are also correct, confirming once again Thomas Hobbes' conclusion that the natural state of man is a state of war. This would not compel men to embrace the human or social model that the zoology of aggression seems to necessitate. Some men will always resent being conformed to the likeness of rats in cages, and it is this quality of man that marks, above all, his religious proclivity. Obviously, for men to embrace by choice the model of the nonviolent man does not hold out to them any guarantee of success, any assured steering of the human future away from catastrophe. It does mean, however, that while men must die, there is open to them, nevertheless, the determination of how and in what name they are to experience death. This option would exist even if there were not a pacific Christ in whose likeness a new humanity could be projected.

NOTES

CHAPTER 1

1. Jean Genet, in *Ramparts,* June 1970, p. 31.
2. *New York Times,* 24 July 1970.
3. *Newsweek,* 12 October 1970, p. 49.
4. Lamentations 2:6 may be counted the one exception.
5. Joseph Klausner, *Jesus of Nazareth,* p. 206; Robert Eisler, *IESOUS BASILEUS OU BASILEUSAS,* 2:88, *The Messiah Jesus and John the Baptist,* p. 264; Joel Carmichael, *The Death of Jesus,* p. 165; S. G. F. Brandon, *Jesus and the Zealots,* pp. 88, n. 4; 200, n. 5 (The statement "it is not clear whether they are commended or condemned," can be defended only by reading Luke's idea into Matthew); p. 300, n. 5.
6. Gottlieb Schrenk, "biazomai, biastēs," *Theological Dictionary of the New Testament,* 1:609–14; W. G. Kümmel, *Promise and Fulfillment,* p. 122.
7. Albert Schweitzer's famous view (*The Quest of the Historical Jesus,* p. 357) of Matthew 11:12, "It is the host of penitents which are wringing it from God, so that it may come now at any moment," still commands attention and is given an altered sense in Julius Schniewind, *Das Evangelium nach Matthäus,* pp. 144–45. There are a dozen other interpretations.
8. Hugh Davis Graham and Ted Robert Gurr, *Violence in America,* p. xxx.
9. Stokely Carmichael and Charles Hamilton, *Black Power,* pp. 4–5.
10. Franz Fanon, *The Wretched of the Earth,* pp. 35–106.

11. Colin Morris, *Unyoung, Uncoloured, Unpoor,* p. 97.

12. Charles West, *Ethics, Violence and Revolution,* pp. 14–15.

13. Jacques Ellul, *Violence,* pp. 27–79.

14. Willis Elliott, in *Renewal,* October 1968, pp. 3–7.

15. Le Roi Jones, *Home,* p. 202.

16. Graham and Gurr, *Violence in America,* p. 66.

17. Henry G. Liddell and Robert Scott, *A Greek-English Lexicon,* I, p. 121.

18. Hugh Schonfield, *The Passover Plot,* p. 190.

19. G. Quispel, in *New Testament Studies,* 5:279. He ascribes "sword, war" to a double transplation of the Aramaic "ḥarba."

20. Trans. by Bruce M. Metzger in Kurt Aland, *Synopsis Quattuor Evangeliorum,* p. 519.

21. Morris, *Unyoung,* p. 24.

22. Ibid. There were 24 people at the Rastenburg headquarters in East Prussia when the bomb exploded at 12:50 P.M. on 20 July 1944. Berger, the stenographer, was killed instantly. General Schmundt, General Korten, and Colonel Brandt died from injuries. General Bodenschatz and Colonel Borgmann were severely wounded. Hitler, by a slight change in the position of von Stauffenberg's lethal briefcase effected by a push from Colonel Brandt's foot, received only minor injury. John W. Wheeler-Bennett, *The Nemesis of Power,* pp. 635–46.

23. Ibid., p. 151.

24. Adolf A. Berle, *Power,* p. 554.

25. Ibid., pp. 439–40.

26. Ibid., p. 30.

27. Tad Szulc and Karl Meyer, *The Cuban Invasion,* p. 110; Theodore Sorenson, *Kennedy,* p. 307; Arthur Schlesinger, Jr., *A Thousand Days,* pp. 25–52.

28. Berle, *Power,* p. 499.

29. Paul Ramsey, in *Dialog,* 6:19–29. David Little, "Is the War in Vietnam Just?" *Reflection,* 64:1–5. Arthur Bud Ogle, "Mister Little— The Answer is 'No!'" *Reflection* 64:1–4; and Paul Ramsey, "From Princeton, With Love," *Reflection* 64:5–6, stood to the right of Little on Vietnam. Little, "Six on Vietnam," *Worldview,* 13:6–11, still spoke of how difficult the difficult questions really are. Reinhold Niebuhur in *Christianity and Crisis,* 26:125–26; 26:221–22; 26:313–14, John C. Bennett (in *Christianity and Crisis,* 26:13–14) editorialized on a statement of Ramsey's regarding Niebuhr's opposition to the war in Vietnam, in which Ramsey wrote, "Even Reinhold Niebuhr signs petitions and editorials as if Reinhold Niebuhr never existed."

CHAPTER 2

1. Rudolf Bultmann, *Jesus*, p. 8.
2. Albert Schweitzer, *The Quest of the Historical Jesus*, p. 333.
3. R. C. Briggs, *Interpreting the Gospels*, p. 135.
4. For example, S. G. F. Brandon, *Jesus and the Zealots*, pp. 78, 257, 259, 281, 334, 339.
5. Ibid., p. 339.
6. Ibid., p. 339, n. 3.
7. Alexander Berendts, *Die Zeugnisse von Christentum im slavischen "De Bello judaico" des Josephus*.
8. Flavius Josephus, 3:648–50; H. St. J. Thackeray, trans., "The Ministry, Trial and Crucifixion of 'The Wonder-Worker,'" in *Josephus*, The Leob Classical Library, Cambridge, Mass.: Harvard University Press, 1961. Used by permission. Passage is discussed by Eisler in *IESOUS BASILEUS OU BASILEUSAS*, 2:297–300, and *The Messiah Jesus and John the Baptist*, pp. 383–85.
9. Brandon, *Zealots*, pp. 364–65.
10. Emil Schürer, in *Theologische Literaturzeitung*, 3:265. In *Zealots*, p. 366, Brandon reiterates Berendt's argument once again, without attempting, however, to sustain its original conclusion. The ambiguous character of the *Halosis* thus issues finally in the use Brandon wishes to make of it.
11. Solomon Zeitlin, *Josephus on Jesus*, pp. 23–24.
12. J. M. Creed, in *Harvard Theological Review*, 25:278.
13. Brandon, *Zealots*, pp. 365–66; Arie Rubenstein, in *Journal of Semitic Studies*, 2:329–48.
14. J. W. Jack, *The Historic Christ*, p. 18.
15. W. Foerster, in *Die Religion in Geschichte und Gegenwart*, 3: col. 868.
16. Eisler, *IESOUS BASILEUS*, 2:23–24, 217, 239–40; *Messiah Jesus*, pp. 356–57.
17. Adolf Schlatter, *Geschichte Israels von Alexander dem Grossen bis Hadrian*, p. 264; *Der Evangelist Matthäus*, p. 350; Martin Hengel, *Die Zeloten*, p. 266.
18. Hengel, in *Journal of Semitic Studies*, 14:231–40.
19. Schlatter, *Der Evangelist Matthäus*, pp. 111–12, 649, 662.
20. Eisler, *IESOUS BASILEUS*, 2:210–18, 243; *Messiah Jesus*, pp. 340–44, 358.
21. Eisler, *IESOUS BASILEUS*, 2:216–17; *Messiah Jesus*, pp. 343–44.
22. Eisler, *IESOUS BASILEUS*, 2:254–70; *Messiah Jesus*, pp. 363–70. This is patently a Schweitzerian adaptation.

23. Eisler, *IESOUS BASILEUS*, 2:280, 508; *Messiah Jesus*, pp. 375, 500.

24. On Matt. 5:41, see Brandon, *Zealots*, p. 202, n. 5.

25. Maurice Goguel, in *Revue historique*, 142:266–67.

26. Hans Jonas, in a hermeneutics lecture at the University of Toronto, on "Permanence and Change," 15 October 1970.

27. Pamphili Eusebius, *Ecclesiastical History*, III, v, 3, in *The Ecclesiastical History and Martyrs of Palestine*, p. 68.

28. Brandon, *Zealots*, p. 211. This passage is discussed in Brandon, *The Fall of Jerusalem and the Christian Church* (pp. 167–69), where it is also mistranslated. On p. 170 of *Fall of Jerusalem*, Brandon connects "before the war" with the time the oracle was given.

29. Walter Wink, in *Union Seminary Quarterly Review*, 25:42, n. 16.

30. Brandon, in *Modern Churchman*, N.S. 8:154.

31. Samuel Sandmel, *The First Christian Century in Judaism and Christianity*, p. 190.

32. W. D. Davies, "The Apostolic Age and the Life of Paul," in *Peake's Commentary on the Bible*, sec. 761d.

33. H. J. Schoeps, in *Journal of Ecclesiastical History*, 3:102. In *Jewish Christianity* (p. 22, n. 7), Schoeps wrote, "The attempt recently made by S. G. F. Brandon and Georg Strecker to treat the flight to Pella as unhistorical is so absurd that I will not discuss it." See also Schoeps, *Theologie und Geschichte des Judenchristentums*, pp. 242–47.

34. Brandon, *Fall of Jerusalem*, pp. 217–48; in *Modern Churchman*, N.S. 8:152–61; *Zealots*, p. 164.

35. Krister Stendahl, "Matthew," in *Peake's Commentary*, sec. 769.

36. Brandon, *Zealots*, p. 307.

37. Arnold Ehrhardt, *The Framework of New Testament Stories*, pp. 174–75; *The Acts of the Apostles*, pp. 101–2. Walter Bauer, *Rechtgläubigkeit und Ketzerei im ältestum Christentum*.

38. Cf. Brandon, *The Trial of Jesus of Nazareth*, pp. 17–23.

39. Brandon, in *Hibbert Journal*, 49:41–47.

40. Brandon, *Fall of Jerusalem*, p. 140.

41. Hans Conzelmann, *Der erste Brief an die Korinther*, pp. 48–49.

42. W. Schmithals, *Paul and James*, p. 103, n. 2.

43. See Brandon, in *Hibbert Journal*, 49:152; C. F. Evans, in *Journal of Theological Studies*, N.S. 7:25–41; Philipp Vielhauer, *Studies in Luke-Acts*, pp. 33–50.

44. Davies, *The Setting of the Sermon on the Mount*, p. 78.

45. Benjamin W. Bacon, *Is Mark a Roman Gospel?*, p. 39.

46. Bertil Gärtner, *The Theology of the Gospel According to Thomas*, p. 66.

47. Helmut Koester, in *Harvard Theological Review*, 58:296.

48. Ibid., p. 291. G. Quispel, in *Vigiliae Christianae*, 16:121–53; in *Journal of Biblical Literature*, 88:321–33. A. F. J. Klijn, *Edessa*, pp. 8, 66–70.

49. Brandon also assumes the priority of Mark. On W. R. Farmer, *The Synoptic Problem*, see Frank W. Beare's review in *Journal of Biblical Literature*, 64:292–97. B. H. Streeter dated Q at A.D. 50 (*The Four Gospels*, p. 150).

50. Matthew's sequence of the three temptations seems preferable. Perhaps Luke alters the sequence out of keeping with his scheme of salvation history that has Jerusalem (cf. Acts) in a time line posterior to the Gospel. Cf. Conzelmann, *The Theology of St. Luke*, p. 27.

51. Brandon, *Zealots*, p. 310.

52. Ibid., p. 314.

53. Ernst Lohmeyer, *Das Evangelium des Markus*, p. 28. Likewise, Ernst Haenchen, *Der Weg Jesu*, pp. 64–65.

54. Brandon, *Zealots*, pp. 310–15.

55. Bultmann, *History of the Synoptic Tradition*, p. 52.

56. Brandon, *Zealots*, p. 314.

57. Bultmann, *Synoptic Tradition*, p. 257.

58. Ibid., p. 258.

59. Bultmann, *Theology of the New Testament*, 1:27.

60. Schlatter, *Der Evangelist Matthäus*, pp. 111–12.

61. Oscar Cullmann, *Jesus and the Revolutionaries*, pp. 39–42.

62. Stendahl, *Peake's Commentary*, sec. 677e.

63. Cf. John 18:11.

64. Colin Morris, *Unyoung, Uncoloured, Unpoor*, p. 119–20.

65. Paradoxically, it is out of his participation in the French resistance during World War II that Ellul wrote of the futile reciprocity and repetitiousness of violence in *Violence*, pp. 96, 102.

66. Brandon, *Trial of Jesus of Nazareth*, p. 32.

67. Yigael Yadin, *Masada*, pp. 197–203.

68. Oriana Fallaci, in *Life*, 12 June 1970, p. 34. George Habash, a physician, resigned from a private clinic which he operated with a group of nuns in Amman in order to become head of the PFLP, and is reported himself to be a Christian.

69. In less than an hour, four Lebanese villages had been bombed by the Israelis, killing 13 and wounding 22 (*New York Times*, 23 May 1970).

146   NOTES

70. Arnold Ehrhardt (*The Framework of New Testament Stories,*
p. 85, n. 2) scores Josephus as "both dishonest and slipshod." To consider, however, the accuracy of Josephus, see Yadin, *Masada,* pp. 201,
226.
71. Josephus, *Antiquities,* 18:8–9.

CHAPTER 3
1. S. G. F. Brandon, *The Fall of Jerusalem,* pp. 204–5; in *New
Testament Studies,* 7:131–32; *Jesus and the Zealots,* pp. 227–29; *The
Trial of Jesus of Nazareth,* p. 70. Cf. Josephus, *War,* 7:153–62.
2. Brandon, *Trial of Jesus,* p. 76.
3. H. J. Schoeps, *Theologie und Geschichte des Judenchristentums,* p. 241.
4. Robert Eisler, *IESOUS BASILEUS OU BASILEUSAS,* 1:371;
The Messiah Jesus and John the Baptist, pp. 146, 149. Eisler ascribed the
passage to Christian redaction (in two phases).
5. Brandon, *Zealots,* p. 228, n. 1; Erich Dinkler, in *Interpreter's
Dictionary of the Bible,* E–J:573.
6. William Sanday and A. C. Headlam, *The Epistle to the Romans,*
p. 87; Otto Michel, *Der Brief an die Römer,* p. 92.
7. Anders Nygren, *Commentary on Romans,* p. 156.
8. Rudolf Bultmann, *Theology of the New Testament,* 1:46.
Bultmann holds, however, that the phrase "to be received by faith"
belongs to Paul's own hand.
9. George Howard, in *Harvard Theological Review,* 63:223–33.
10. R. H. Lightfoot, *The Gospel Message of St. Mark,* pp. 55–56.
11. Lake and Cadbury, *The Beginnings of Christianity,* 5:220. Hans
Conzelmann, *The Theology of St. Luke,* p. 197, n. 3; C. H. Talbert, *Luke
and the Gnostics,* p. 71: "the death of Jesus in Luke-Acts is not connected with the forgiveness of sins as it is in Paul's writings and in the
other Synoptics."
12. Vincent Taylor (*Behind the Third Gospel,* p. 58) is assured that
Luke 23:44–45 derives from Mark and not Proto-Luke (if one holds to
Proto-Luke).
13. Cf. C. E. B. Cranfield, in *Interpreter's Dictionary,* K–Q:267–68.
14. Cf. W. G. Kümmel, *Introduction to the New Testament,* p. 68.
15. C. F. Evans, *The Beginnings of the Gospel,* p. 71.
16. Ernst Lohmeyer, *Galiläa und Jerusalem.*
17. Willi Marxsen, *Introduction to the New Testament,* p. 68.
18. L. E. Elliott-Binns, *Galilean Christianity,* ch. 1 in particular.
Lightfoot, *Locality and Doctrine in the Gospels,* chs. 3, 5.

19. Cf. Acts 5:37. The chronology of Luke 2:2 and Acts 5:36–37 cannot be defended.

20. Josephus, *War* 2:118. Chapters 2 and 3 of Brandon, *Zealots,* focus on this issue.

21. Ernst Haenchen, *Der Weg Jesu,* p. 408.

22. Brandon, *Trial of Jesus,* p. 67; cf. *Zealots,* pp. 224, 270–71, 345–49. Brandon's earlier position on Mark 12:17 was more modest: "Consequently on fair analysis we learn nothing here of the attitude of Jesus toward Jewish nationalism, unless it is the negative conclusion that he astutely avoided the issue" ("The Logic of New Testament Criticism," *Hibbert Journal,* 47:147).

23. Eisler, *Messiah Jesus,* pp. 334–35.

24. Colin Morris, *Unyoung, Uncoloured, Unpoor,* p. 113.

25. Bultmann, *History of the Synoptic Tradition,* p. 40.

26. Ibid., p. 26.

27. Brandon, *Fall of Jerusalem,* p. 191. The phraseology in Brandon, *Zealots* (p. 341, n. 1), is unfortunately altered to read: "If Bultmann is right. . . ."

28. C. G. Montefiore, *The Synoptic Gospels,* 1:279.

29. Israel Abrahams, *Studies in Pharisaism and the Gospels,* 1:62–65.

30. Ibid., p. 63.

31. Shabbat 16.8 of the Babylonian Talmud. Quoted by W. Bacher in *The Jewish Encyclopedia,* 7:214.

32. For the various views see Jacob Neusner, *A Life of Rabban Johanan ben Zakkai,* p. 29, n. 2.

33. Yoma 39b. I. Epstein, ed., *The Babylonian Talmud,* Pt. 2/V, p. 186.

34. Brandon, *Zealots,* pp. 209, n. 1, 215. Gittin 56a-b, *The Babylonian Talmud,* Pt. 3/III, pp. 257–58.

35. See Neusner, *Life of Rabban ben Zakkai,* pp. 104–79.

36. Ernst Käsemann, *New Testament Questions for Today,* p. 216. C. H. Dodd, *The Epistle of Paul to the Romans,* p. 103, found in Romans 13:6–7 a definite awareness on Paul's part of the apothegm in Mark 12:17 and an anti-Zealot polemic in Romans 13:2, further argument for the pre-Markan character of the pronouncement. For recent discussion of the relation between the sayings of Jesus and the teachings of Paul, see Victor Paul Furnish, *Theology and Ethics in Paul,* pp. 51–67.

37. An impressive exception is James Douglass, *The Non-violent Cross,* pp. 217–82.

38. Brandon, *Zealots,* pp. 10, 243–45.

39. Ibid., p. 201, n. 4.

40. This is the brunt of Barth's position in Karl Barth and Johannes Hamel, *How to Serve God in a Marxist Land.*

41. Station CBL in Toronto.

42. John R. Colombo, in *The Canadian Forum*, July 1960, p. 80.

43. *New York Times*, 23 October 1966.

44. Morton Smith, in *Harvard Theological Review*, 64:1–19.

45. Jackson and Lake, *Beginnings of Christianity*, 1:421–25. Cf. the discussion in Brandon, *Fall of Jerusalem*, p. 105, n. 1. Josephus, *War*, 4:130–61, describes the formation of the Zealot party during the war.

46. Günther Baumbach, in *Theologische Literaturzeitung*, 90:727–40.

47. Jackson and Lake, *Beginnings of Christianity*, 1:425.

48. Paul Winter, *On the Trial of Jesus*, p. 140.

49. Brandon, *Trial of Jesus*, p. 104.

50. Constantin Daniel, in *Numen*, 13:97. Daniel finds reference by paronomasia to Zealot whenever reed (*kalamos*) occurs in Matthew. "Bruised reed" thus in Matthew 12:20 means a Zealot, but "smoldering wick" means an Essene!

51. In modern Israel a Jew named Cohen cannot lawfully marry a divorced woman, because theoretically Cohens (once a priest, always a priest) may one day be called upon to officiate in a new temple. So Uri Avnery, *Israel Without Zionists*, p. 159.

52. *Journal of Semitic Studies*, 14:236.

53. Günther Bornkamm, *Jesus of Nazareth*, pp. 73–74, 78–82, 97–98.

54. W. R. Farmer, in *Christian History and Interpretation*, pp. 101–126.

55. Erik H. Erikson, *Gandhi's Truth*, p. 266.

56. Brandon, *Zealots*, p. 9, n. 4; p. 333, n. 3.

57. Ibid., p. 338.

58. Ibid., pp. 9, 333, 338.

59. Ibid., pp. 333–34.

60. Ibid., p. 237.

61. Ibid., p. 238.

62. Ibid., p. 342.

63. Other allusions are in Mark 15:29 (same as Matt. 27:40), Acts 6:14.

64. Brandon, *Zealots*, pp. 331, n. 5; 314, 334.

65. Ibid., p. 234.

66. Lloyd Gaston (*No Stone on Another*, pp. 4–5, 96–99, 243–44,

etc.) attempts to show that Jesus and the primitive church denigrated the temple cultus, especially sacrifices, but not the temple itself.

67. Brandon, *Zealots*, p. 252.

68. Ibid., p. 251.

69. Conzelmann, in *Interpretation*, 24:187.

70. Brandon, *Zealots*, p. 333.

71. Counting from Kurt Aland, *Synopsis Quattuor Evangeliorum*, p. 372.

72. T. W. Manson, *The Servant-Messiah*, pp. 81–83.

73. So most commentators. Cf. Lohmeyer, *Das Evangelium Markus*, pp. 236–37. Paul Winter (*On the Trial of Jesus*, p. 143) locates the episode in a "corner" of the Court of the Gentiles; it was perhaps "little more than a brawl in an Eastern bazaar."

74. Josephus, *War*, 5:194; *Antiquities*, 15:417. See Brandon, *Zealots*, p. 237, n. 4.

75. Cf. Ferdinand Hahn, *Mission in the New Testament*, pp. 114–15.

76. Edwin C. Hoskyns, *The Fourth Gospel*, 1:203.

77. Bultmann, *Das Evangelium des Johannes*, p. 86, n. 10. The objection expressed by Schnackenburg (*The Gospel According to St. John*, 1:346) that "all" (*pantas*) cannot refer to the animals because it occurs in the masculine gender (hence must refer to the merchants) is incorrect, as pointed out in A. Loisy, *Le Quatrième Évangile*, p. 287. "Sheep" (*probata*) is neuter; "cattle" (*boas*) is masculine. The modifier *may* follow the nearer substantive, but the masculine may also dominate over both feminine and neuter. See A. T. Robertson, *A Grammar of the Greek New Testament in the Light of Historical Research*, p. 655, and E. C. Colwell, *The Greek of the Fourth Gospel*, p. 121.

78. G. H. C. Macgregor, *The Gospel of John*, p. 58.

79. Cf. Reginald H. Fuller, *Foundations of New Testament Christology*, p. 234.

80. It is not impossible further to relate "the birds of the air" in Psalm 8:8 (Hebrew verse 9) to the pigeons of John 2:16.

81. Bultmann, *Das Evangelium des Johannes*, p. 86.

82. Raymond Brown, *The Gospel According to John*, 1:115.

83. B. F. Westcott, *The Gospel According to St. John*, 1:91.

84. On the possibility that the cleansing of the Temple is moved in the fourth Gospel from the final week of Jesus' ministry to the initial phase of it (reversing the synoptic chronology) on account of the suddenness of the Lord's coming in Malachi 3:1, cf. Brown, *The Gospel According to John*, 1:118. Eisler ascribes the change of chronological position to

the desire of John to conceal the connection between "the fatal riot in the Temple" and the Roman charge against Jesus eventuating in the crucifixion (*The Enigma of the Fourth Gospel*, p. 176). If Eisler is correct, it is another case of John altering what he felt to be a misuse (i.e., mistakenly political) of this tradition.

85. Ellul, *Violence*, p. 17. Ellul correctly deplores the baleful use of the tradition, while perpetuating at the same time an exegetical anomaly that has made such misuse possible.

86. Cuin H. Felder, in *Union Seminary Quarterly Review*, 25:545.

CHAPTER 4

1. These summary remarks on William Wrede are derived from Georg Strecker, in *Zeitschrift für Theologie und Kirche*, 57:67–91.

2. Adapted from Willi Marxsen, *Introduction to the New Testament*, p. 136.

3. Wrede, *Das Messiasgeheimnis*, pp. 116–17.

4. Ibid., p. 120.

5. Ibid., pp. 120–21.

6. Ibid., p. 16.

7. Ibid., pp. 126–27.

8. Ibid., pp. 227–28. Cf. Acts 2:36, Rom. 1:4, Phil. 2:6–11.

9. K. L. Schmidt, *Der Rahmen der Geschichte Jesu*, pp. v–ix.

10. Ibid., p. 50.

11. Rudolf Bultmann, *History of the Synoptic Tradition*, p. 212.

12. Hans J. Ebeling, *Das Messiasgeheimnis und die Botschaft des Marcusevangelisten*, pp. 137–38.

13. James M. Robinson, *The Problem of History in Mark*, p. 39.

14. Helmut Koester, in *Verkündigung und Forschung*, p. 182. Robinson responded in *Union Seminary Quarterly Review*, 20:131–47.

15. See Krister Stendahl, *The School of St. Matthew*, pp. 11–13, 204; G. Bornkamm, G. Barth, and H. J. Held, *Tradition and Interpretation in Matthew*, pp. 125–28.

16. Wrede (*Das Messiasgeheimnis*. p. 145) said, "Is the idea of the messianic secret the discovery of Mark? That is a notion entirely improbable." But cf. Albert Schweitzer, *The Quest of the Historical Jesus*, p. 339.

17. Martin Dibelius, *From Tradition to Gospel*, p. 230.

18. So H. E. Tödt, *Son of Man in the Synoptic Tradition*, p. 132, against B. H. Boobyer, in *New Testament Studies*, 6:27–28.

19. Martin Kähler, *The So-Called Historical Jesus and the Historic, Biblical Christ*, p. 80, n. 11.

20. Eta Linnemann, in *Zeitschrift für Theologie und Kirche,* 66:255–87; Kurt Aland, in *Zeitschrift für Theologie und Kirche,* 67:3–13.

21. R. H. Lightfoot, *The Gospel Message of St. Mark,* pp. 80–97, 106–16.

22. Wilhelm Bousset, *Kyrios Christos,* pp. 70, 80–81.

23. David Daube, *The New Testament and Rabbinic Judaism,* pp. 158–69. "The Markan section . . . betrays the immediate influence of the Passover-eve recital. Very likely, it came into existence, or at any rate was published, on the occasion of a Jewish-Christian Seder" (p. 168). Cf. Francis W. Beare, *The Earliest Records of Jesus,* p. 211.

24. Lightfoot, *The Gospel Message,* pp. 49–58; Charles Cousar, in *Interpretation,* 24:321–35.

25. Georg Strecker (in *Interpretation,* 22:421–43) held that the first prediction belongs to the pre-Markan tradition, while the latter two are Markan elaborations of 8:31. Cf., on the other hand, Ernst Haenchen, in *Novum Testamentum,* 6:81–100, and N. Perrin, in *Journal of Religion,* 46:298.

26. Robert Grant, *Historical Introduction to the New Testament,* p. 123, slightly emended.

27. Ulrich Luz (in *Zeitschrift für die neutestamentliche Wissenschaft,* 56:15) says on 8:22–26, "So the account may not be a miracle story but a symbolic description of the healing of the blindness of men through Jesus. . . ."

28. Heinz-Dieter Knigge, in *Interpretation,* 22:68–69. Cf. J. Schreiber, in *Zeitschrift für Theologie und Kirche,* 58:159–60. The John/Jesus analogue obviously informs Luke 1 and 2, which led Conzelmann (*The Theology of St. Luke*) to separate radically between Luke 1–2 and the rest of Luke where John and Jesus belong to two different "worlds." Mark has no qualms about parallels between John and Jesus. Could Luke have abandoned the parallel because of political overtones which became joined to John's ministry?—a doubtful possibility. But if it were so, Mark does not sense the embarrassment.

29. L. E. Keck, in *Journal of Biblical Literature,* 84:341–58, argued that 3:7–12 belongs to the section beginning at 1:16. In treating Mark's christology (the divine man overshadowed by the cross), Keck and Eduard Schweizer (against J. Schreiber, in *Zeitschrift für Theologie und Kirche,* 58:154–83) come to similar conclusions.

30. Joachim Jeremias, *The Parables of Jesus,* pp. 77–79.

31. Schweizer, in *Zeitschrift für die neutestamentliche Wissenschaft,* 56:5, has maintained (with Jeremias) that 4:11–12 are part

of the pre-Markan tradition, belonging perhaps to an Isaiah Targum.
  32. Cf. Col. 4:5; 1 Tim. 3:7.
  33. Marxsen (*Mark the Evangelist*, p. 39, n. 33) points out how "arrest" or "betray" (*paradidonai*) is used in the absolute sense only of Jesus in 3:19, 14:11, 18, 21, 42, 15:10, and variant readings of 14:10. Additional descriptive information is supplied when the verb is used of other persons (e.g., 13:9 and 12). The one exception to this is 1:14, i.e., of John.
  34. Keck, in *Journal of Biblical Literature*, 84:345, n. 30.
  35. Marxsen, *Mark the Evangelist*, pp. 117–50; *Introduction to the New Testament*, pp. 137–38.
  36. Conzelmann, in *Zeitschrift für Theologie und Kirche*, 54:294.
  37. Helmut Koester, in *Harvard Theological Review*, 61:233, n. 105.
  38. Schweizer, *The Good News According to Mark*, p. 383, cf. pp. 23–24. (Matthew and Luke do so only derivatively.)
  39. Conzelmann, in *Zeitschrift für Theologie und Kirche*, 64:295. Since Mark alone really employs the Secret, his Gospel is not "one of a kind" but "the only one of its kind." Cf. Marxsen, *Mark the Evangelist*, p. 150, n. 109.
  40. Albert Schweitzer, *The Mystery of the Kingdom of God*, pp. 5–6.
  41. Bultmann, *Theology of the New Testament*, 1:27.
  42. Hugh Schonfield, *The Passover Plot*, pp. 64–69, 77, 98, 184.
  43. A. Dupont-Sommer, *The Essene Writings from Qumran*, translated by G. Vermès, pp. 187–88, 1QM xii: 10–14. Oxford: Basil Blackwell, 1961 (New York: The World Publishing Company, 1962). Translation Copyright © 1962 by The World Publishing Company. Reprinted by permission.
  44. 1QSa ii:14–15, trans. Helmer Ringgren, *The Faith of Qumran*, p. 170. Also see T. H. Gaster, *The Dead Sea Scriptures*, p. 329.
  45. Bultmann, *Theology of the New Testament*, 1:29–31, is followed in these details.
  46. Streeter, *The Four Gospels*, p. 322. Also, John Knox, *The Death of Christ*, pp. 79–81.
  47. The history of the controversy is cogently restated by N. A. Dahl in *Christian History and Interpretation*, pp. 313–15.
  48. Conzelmann, in *Interpretation*, 22:181.
  49. U. Wilckens, *Weisheit und Torheit*, p. 17.
  50. Ibid., p. 20.
  51. Conzelmann, in *Interpretation*, 22:181.

52. Ibid., p. 70.

53. Schweizer, in *New Testament Studies*, 10:432.

54. Keck, in *Journal of Biblical Literature*, 84:357.

55. Jeremias, *The Parables of Jesus*, p. 16. Also Marxsen, in *Zeitschrift für Theologie und Kirche*, 52:256–57, 264. Marxsen goes further than Jeremias in explaining Mark's idea by appeal to *māshāl*.

56. Mark's awareness through the tradition of the prophetic ethic is as clear in the passage on the deceitfulness of riches in Mark 10:17–27 (in a negative sense) as it is in the teaching on the Great Commandment in Mark 12:28–34 (in a positive sense). In Mark 7:1–23, ritual propriety is contrasted with radical obedience from the inmost self with Isaiah 29:13 (Mark 7:6–7) as Mark's prooftext. Mark 7:14–23 recapitulates 4:1–20 so neatly that it must also reflect Mark's arrangement. So Marxsen, in *Zeitschrift für Theologie und Kirche*, 50:259–63.

57. Cf. Jer. 5:21; Ezek. 12:2. Matthew 13:1–15 broadens the base of Mark's Isaiah allusion.

58. D. E. Nineham, *The Gospel of St. Mark*. pp. 127–28.

59. K. Schubert, *The Dead Sea Community*, p. 68. The ideas on Qumran "knowledge" and the translations cited are from Schubert, ibid., pp. 67–74.

60. For the more direct avenue of contact between Christianity and Gnosticism we must probably look to Nag Hammadi; cf. Robinson, in *New Testament Studies*, 14:372–80.

61. Trans. Metzger, in Kurt Aland, *Synopsis Quattuor Evangeliorum*, p. 527.

62. Paul Tillich, *Theology of Culture*, pp. 30–39.

63. Brandon, *Jesus and the Zealots*, p. 145.

64. Walter Wink, in *Union Seminary Quarterly Review*, 25:58.

CHAPTER 5

1. George H. Mead, *Mind, Self and Society*, pp. 135–226, esp. pp. 144–49.

2. H. L. Nieburg, *Political Violence*, pp. 138–39.

3. Erich Fromm, *The Crisis of Psychotherapy*, p. 25. Fromm (pp. 1–29) holds that Freud opened the possibility either of a reformist or a radical future for psychotherapy, depending, for example, on whether "false consciousness" were applied to economic and political as well as sexual experience. The confinement of psychotherapy to the latter domain compromised the radical possibilities of Freud.

4. There is a legend that when Hitler flew over Poland to view
the damage resulting from the German conquest in 1939, he broke into
tears and said, "How foolish of you Poles to make me do this to you!"
At the height of the invasion of Laos on 9 March 1971, Mr. Nixon
described himself as a "deeply committed pacifist." He wisely added,
"It is not enough just to be for peace. The point is, what can we do
about it" (*New York Times*, 10 March 1971).

5. John Yoder, *Karl Barth and the Problem of War*, p. 136, n. 3.

6. Rudolf Bultmann, in *Christianity and Crisis*, 75:969. In August of 1964, through the kind auspices of Mrs. Franz Claassen of Göttingen, I was privileged to talk with Professor Bultmann while he was
vacationing with his wife and daughter (Mrs. Lemke) in the Black
Forest. He reiterated again his familiar reservations about the peace
movement, particularly the fact that people may become enthused
about political movements without making a serious existential decision
leading them to authenticity. The criticism was a statement of fact and
not, as I understood it, a broadside attack on the peace movement.
As to the church's ability or the Christian's ability to make political
decisions, Bultmann expressed in good humor his hope that "America
wouldn't elect Goldwater president." I asked him how he felt competent to express such an opinion. He remained silent. He referred
specifically to the article, "Theology for Freedom and Responsibility,"
indicating his continued advocacy of its content six years after its
publication.

7. See Yoder, *Karl Barth*, pp. 133–37.

8. Cf. Arthur Cochrane, *The Church's Confession under Hitler*.

9. *New York Times*, 6 June 1945, p. 11.

10. *New York Times*, 28 July 1968, p. 1.

11. Reinhold Niebuhr, *Christianity and Power Politics*, p. 10.

12. H. Richard Niebuhr, *Christ and Culture*, p. 45.

13. Roland Bainton, *Christian Attitudes Toward War and Peace*,
p. 14.

14. Ibid., p. 77.

15. Reinhold Niebuhr, *An Interpretation of Christian Ethics*, pp.
44–48; *Christianity and Power Politics*, pp. 8–11.

16. H. Richard Niebuhr, *The Responsible Self*, p. 19.

17. James M. Gustafson, *Christ and the Moral Life*, p. 205, n. 21.

18. H. Richard Niebuhr, *The Responsible Self*, p. 68.

19. Gustafson, in *Interpretation*, 24:452.

20. Ibid., p. 437. An SDS film on the sad events attending the

1968 Democratic convention in Chicago refers in one place to "killing a cop for the sake of love." This is shocking only to those who do not want to see how applicable to many elements of churchly mentality today is the slogan "Kill a Commie for Christ."

21. These features were first brought to my attention in a lecture by John H. Yoder at the Southern Baptist Theological Seminary in Louisville, Kentucky, on 6 May 1970.

22. H. Richard Niebuhr, *Christ and Culture*, p. 46.

23. Ibid., p. 48.

24. Ibid., p. 32.

25. Ibid., p. 48.

26. Toronto *Globe and Mail*, 17 June 1971, p. 10.

27. Jacques Ellul, *Violence*, p. 84. Also see Ellul, *Political Illusion*, pp. 71–77.

28. William Stringfellow, in *Christianity and Crisis*, 30:183.

29. *Christianity and Power Politics*, pp. 1–23.

30. Cf. Paul Ramsey, in *Worldview*, 10:8–11.

31. The opprobrium that the Christian majority has associated with the much abused term "pacifist" was now directed by the commission against those who have dignified the just war theory by such pleasant adjectives as "realistic" and "responsible."

32. Quoted from excerpts of the report, *New York Times*, 5 March 1967, p. 82.

33. *New York Times*, 9 March 1971, p. 20.

34. Ibid.

35. Ralph Potter (*War and Moral Discourses*, p. 59) ascribes the excesses of World War II to the baleful influence of pacifists, who thwarted, between the two World Wars, the development of adequate guidelines for determining the acceptable limits of violence in war!

36. This shameful story is told by Arthur D. Morse, *While Six Million Died*.

37. C. Wright Mills, *The Causes of World War III*, p. 62.

38. German Guzman, *Camilo Torres*, p. 77.

39. *Violence in Southern Africa*, p. 76.

40. Cf. Albert Luthuli, *Let My People Go*.

41. *Violence in Southern Africa*, pp. 76–77.

42. J. A. Ryan and F. J. Boland, *Catholic Principles of Politics*, p. 255.

43. Cf. James C. Smylie, in *Journal of Church and Society*, 11:383–408. The Christian debate on Vietnam raises the question how

unjust does a war have to be to be declared unjust by official ecclesiastical action. Practically speaking, the chaplaincy will see to it that no such official action is taken.

44. Bultmann and K. Kundsin, *Form Criticism*, pp. 72–73.

45. James M. Gustafson, in the Introduction to H. Richard Niebuhr, *The Responsible Self*, p. 19.

46. Ibid., p. 31.

47. Bultmann, *Theology in the New Testament*, 1:260–61.

48. Gutafson, *Christ and the Moral Life*, p. 158.

49. Robert Ardrey, *African Genesis, The Territorial Imperative, The Social Contract*, Konrad Lorenz *On Aggression*.

50. Thomas Merton, *Faith and Violence*, pp. 96–105.

51. Nieburg, *Political Violence*, p. 39.

52. Hannah Arendt, *On Violence*, pp. 61–62.

53. Ardrey, *African Genesis*, pp. 272–82.

54. M. F. Ashley-Montagu, *Man and Aggression*, pp. 3–17.

BIBLIOGRAPHY OF WORKS CITED

Abrahams, Isaac. *Studies in Pharisaism and the Gospels.* 2 series. Cambridge: University Press, 1917, 1921.

Aland, Kurt, ed. *Synopsis Quattuor Evangeliorum.* 2d ed. Stuttgart: Württembergische Bibelanstalt, 1964.

——. "Die wiedergefundene Markusschluss?" *Zeitschrift für Theologie und Kirche* 67 (1970) : 3–13.

Ardrey, Robert. *African Genesis.* New York: Atheneum, 1961.

——. *The Social Contract.* New York: Atheneum, 1970.

——. *The Territorial Imperative.* New York: Atheneum, 1966.

Arendt, Hannah. *On Violence.* New York: Harcourt, Brace & World, 1969.

Ashley-Montagu, M. F. *Man and Aggression.* New York: Oxford, 1968.

Avnery, Uri. *Israel Without Zionists.* New York: Macmillan, 1968.

Bacher, W. "Johanan b. Zakkai." In *The Jewish Encyclopedia.* Ed. Isidore Singer. Vol. 7. New York: Funk and Wagnalls, 1904.

Bacon, Benjamin W. *Is Mark a Roman Gospel?* Harvard Theological Studies 7. Cambridge, Mass.: Harvard University Press, 1919.

Bainton, Roland. *Christian Attitudes Toward War and Peace.* New York: Abingdon, 1960.

Barth, Karl, and Hamel, Johannes. *How to Serve God in a Marxist Land.* Trans. Henry Clark, James D. Smart, Thomas Wieser. Intro. R. N. Brown. New York: Association, 1959.

Bauer, Walter. *Rechtgläubigkeit und Ketzerei im ältestum Christentum.* 2d ed. Ed. Georg Strecker. Tübingen: J. C. B. Mohr, 1964.

157

Baumbach, Günther. "Zeloten und Sikarier." *Theologische Literaturzeitung* 90 (1965): 727–40.

Beare, Francis W. *The Earliest Records of Jesus*. Oxford: Basil Blackwell, 1962.

———. Review of *The Synoptic Problem* by W. R. Farmer. *Journal of Biblical Literature* 64 (1965): 292–97.

Bennett, John C. "From Supporter of War in 1941 to Critic in 1966." *Christianity and Crisis* 26 (1966): 13–14.

Berendts, Alexander. *Die Zeugnisse von Christentum im slavischen "De Bello judaico" des Josephus*. Leipzig: J. C. Hinrich, 1906.

Berle, Adolf A. *Power*. 2d ed. New York: Harcourt, Brace & World, 1969.

Black, M., and Rowley, H. H., eds. *Peake's Commentary on the Bible*. 2d ed. New York: Nelson, 1962.

Boobyer, G. H. "Galilee and Galileans in St. Mark's Gospel." *Bulletin of the John Rylands Library* 35 (1952–53): 334–48.

———. "The Secret Motif in St. Mark's Gospel." *New Testament Studies* 6 (1959–60): 225–35.

Bornkamm, Günther. *Jesus of Nazareth*. Trans. Irene & Fraser McLusky, James M. Robinson. New York: Harper & Row, 1960.

———, Barth, G., and Held, H. J. *Tradition and Interpretation in Matthew*. Trans. Percy Scott. New Testament Library. Philadelphia: Westminster, 1963.

Bousset, Wilhelm. *Kyrios Christos*. Trans. John E. Steely. New York: Abingdon, 1970 (first German ed., 1913).

Brandon, S. G. F. "The Crisis of A.D. 70." *Hibbert Journal* 46 (1948): 221–28.

———. "The Date of the Markan Gospel." *New Testament Studies* 7 (1960–61): 126–41.

———. *The Fall of Jerusalem and the Christian Church*. 2d ed. London: SPCK, 1957.

———. *Jesus and the Zealots. A Study of the Political Factor in Primitive Christianity*. New York: Scribner's, 1967.

———. "The Logic of New Testament Criticism." *Hibbert Journal* 47 (1949): 144–52.

———. "The Markan Apocalypse." *Modern Churchman* 44 (1954): 315–324.

———. "Matthaean Christianity." *Modern Churchman* N.S. 8 (1965): 152–61.

———. *The Trial of Jesus of Nazareth*. New York: Stein and Day, 1968.

————. "Tübingen Vindicated?" *Hibbert Journal* 49 (1951): 41–47.

Briggs, R. C. *Interpreting the Gospels*. New York: Abingdon, 1969.

Brown, Raymond. *The Gospel According to John*. The Anchor Bible. 2 vols. Garden City, N. Y.: Doubleday, 1966–70.

Brown, Richard Maxwell. "Historical Patterns of Violence in America." In *Violence in America: Historical and Comparative Perspectives*. Ed. Hugh Davis Graham and Ted Robert Gurr. New York: Bantam, 1969.

Bultmann, Rudolf. *Das Evangelium des Johannes*. 13th ed. Meyers kritisch-exegetischer Kommentar über das Neue Testament. Göttingen: Vandenhoeck & Ruprecht, 1950. English: *The Gospel of John: A Commentary*. Trans. G. R. Beasley-Murray. Ed. R. W. N. Hoare & J. K. Riches. Oxford: Basil Blackwell, 1971.

————. *The History of the Synoptic Tradition*. Trans. John Marsh. Oxford: Basil Blackwell, 1963.

————. *Jesus and the Word*. Trans. Louise Smith & Erminie Lantero. New York: Scribner's, 1958.

————, "Theology for Freedom and Responsibility." *Christian Century* 75 (1958): 967–69.

————. *The Theology of the New Testament*. 2 vols. Trans. K. Grobel. New York: Scribner's, 1951.

————, and Kundsin, K. *Form Criticism*. Trans. F. C. Grant. Chicago: Willett & Clark, 1934.

Buttrick, George A., et al., eds. *The Interpreter's Dictionary of the Bible*. 4 vols. New York: Abingdon, 1962.

Carmichael, Joel. *The Death of Jesus*. New York: Macmillan, 1962.

Carmichael, Stokely, and Hamilton, Charles. *Black Power: The Politics of Liberation*. New York: Vintage, 1967.

Cochrane, Arthur. *The Church's Confession under Hitler*. Philadelphia: Westminster, 1962.

Colombo, John R. "Canada's Banned Poet." *The Canadian Forum* 40 (July 1960): 80–82.

Colwell, E. C. *The Greek of the Fourth Gospel*. Chicago: University of Chicago Press, 1931.

Cone, Arnold. *Black Theology and Black Power*. New York: Seabury, 1969.

Conzelmann, Hans. "Current Problems in New Testament Research." *Interpretation* 22 (1968): 171–86.

————. *Der Erste Brief an die Korinther*. 11th ed. Meyers kritisch-exegetischer Kommentar über das Neue Testament. Göttingen: Vandenhoeck & Ruprecht, 1969.

————. "Gegenwart und Zukunft in der synoptischen Tradition." *Zeit-schrift für Theologie und Kirche* 54 (1957): 277–96.

————. "History and Theology in the Passion Narratives of the Synoptic Gospels." Trans. Chas. B. Cousar. *Interpretation* 24 (1970): 178–197.

————. *The Theology of St. Luke.* Trans. Geoffrey Buswell. London: Faber and Faber, 1960.

Cousar, Charles B. "Eschatology and Mark's Theologia Crucis." *Interpretation* 24 (1970): 321–35.

Cranfield, C. E. B. "Mark, Gospel of." In *Interpreter's Dictionary of the Bible.* Ed. George Buttrick et al. New York: Abingdon, 1962.

Creed, J. M. "The Slavonic Version of Josephus' History of the Jewish War." *Harvard Theological Review* 25 (1932): 277–319.

Cullmann, Oscar. *Jesus and the Revolutionaries.* Trans. Gareth Putnam. New York: Harper & Row, 1970.

————. *The State in the New Testament.* New York: Scribner's, 1956.

Dahl, Nils A. "Paul and the Church at Corinth." In *Christian History and Interpretation: Studies Presented to John Knox.* Ed. W. R. Farmer, C. F. D. Moule, and R. R. Niebuhr. Cambridge: University Press, 1967.

Daniel, Constantin. "Esséniens, zélotes et sicaires et leur mention par paronymie dans le Nouveau Testament." *Numen* 13 (1966): 88–115.

Daube, David. *The New Testament and Rabbinic Judaism.* London: Athlone, 1956.

Davies, W. D. "The Apostolic Age and the Life of Paul." In *Peake's Commentary on the Bible.* 2d ed. Ed. M. Black and H. H. Rowley. New York: Nelson, 1962.

————. *The Setting of the Sermon on the Mount.* Cambridge: University Press, 1964.

Dibelius, Martin. *From Tradition to Gospel.* Trans. Bertram L. Woolf. London: Ivor, Nicholson & Watson, 1934.

————. *The Sermon on the Mount.* New York: Scribner's, 1940.

Dinkler, Erich. "Hebrews, Letter to the." In *Interpreter's Dictionary of the Bible.* Ed. George Buttrick et al. New York: Abingdon, 1962.

Dodd, C. H. *The Epistle of Paul to the Romans.* Moffatt New Testament Commentary. London: Hodder & Stoughton, 1932.

Douglass, James W. *The Non-Violent Cross.* New York: Macmillan, 1966.

Dupont-Sommer, A., *The Essene Writings from Qumran.* Trans. G. Vermès. Oxford: Basil Blackwell, 1961; New York: The World Publishing Company, 1962.

Ebeling, Hans. J. *Das Messiasgeheimnis und die Botschaft des Marcus-Evangelisten*. Zeitschrift für die neutestamentliche Wissenschaft, Beiheft 19. Berlin: Töpelmann, 1939.

Ehrhardt, Arnold. *The Acts of the Apostles*. Manchester: University, 1969.

———. *The Framework of the New Testament Stories*. Manchester: University, 1964.

Eisler, Robert. *The Enigma of the Fourth Gospel*. London: Methuen, 1938.

———. *IESOUS BASILEUS OU BASILEUSAS*. 2 vols. Heidelberg: Carl Winter, 1929–30.

———. *The Messiah Jesus and John the Baptist*. Trans. and rev. Alexander H. Krappe. New York: Dial, 1931.

Elliott, Willis. "No Alternative to Violence." *Renewal* 8 (October 1968): 3–7.

Elliott-Binns, L. E. *Galilean Christianity*. Studies in Biblical Theology 16. London: SCM, 1956.

Ellul, Jacques. *Political Illusion*. Trans. Konrad Kellen. New York: Knopf, 1967.

———. *Violence*. Trans. Cecelia G. Kings. New York: Seabury, 1969.

Epstein, I., ed. *The Babylonian Talmud*. Pt. 2, vol. 5: *Seder Mo'ed*. Trans. Leon Yung. London: Soncino, 1938, Pt. 3, vol. 7: *Seder Nashim*. London: Soncino, 1938.

Erikson, Erik H. *Gandhi's Truth: On the Origins of Militant Nonviolence*. New York: W. W. Norton, 1969.

Eusebius, Pamphili. *Ecclesiastical History and Martyrs of Palestine*. Trans. Hugh H. Lawlor and John E. L. Oulton. 2 vols. London: SPCK, 1927. Greek text of *E. H.* III, v, 3 in *Patrologiae Graecae*. Ed. J. P. Migne. Tom. 20. Paris: Garnier, 1857. Col. 221.

Evans, C. F. *The Beginnings of the Gospel*. London: SPCK, 1968.

———. "The Kerygma." *Journal of Theological Studies* N.S. 7 (1956): 25–41.

Fallaci, Oriana. "A leader of the fedayeen: 'We want a war like the Vietnam War.'" *Life* 79 (June 12, 1970): 33–34.

Fanon, Franz. *The Wretched of the Earth*. Intro. Jean-Paul Sartre. Trans. Constance Farrington. New York: Grove, 1968.

Farmer, W. R. "An Historical Essay on the Humanity of Jesus Christ." In *Christian History and Interpretation: Studies Presented to John Knox*. Ed. W. R. Farmer, C. F. D. Moule, and R. R. Niebuhr. Cambridge: University Press, 1967.

———. *The Synoptic Problem: A Critical Analysis.* New York: Macmillan, 1964.

Felder, Cuin H. Review of *Black Theology and Black Power* by Arnold Cone. *Union Seminary Quarterly Review* 25 (1970): 543–46.

Foerster, W. "Josephus, Flavius." In *Die Religion in Geschichte und Gegenwart.* Ed. Kurt Galling, Bd. 3. Tübingen: J. C. B. Mohr, 1959.

Fromm, Erich. *The Crisis of Psychoanalysis.* New York: Holt, Rinehart, and Winston, 1970.

———. *May Man Prevail?* Garden City, N.Y.: Doubleday, 1961.

Fuller, Reginald H. *Foundations of New Testament Christology.* London: Lutterworth, 1965.

Furnish, Victor Paul. *Theology and Ethics in Paul.* New York: Abingdon, 1968.

Gärtner, Bertil. *The Theology of the Gospel According to Thomas.* Trans. E. J. Sharpe. New York: Harper & Row, 1961.

Galling, Kurt, ed. *Die Religion in Geschichte und Gegenwart.* 3d ed. 7 vols. Tübingen: J. C. B. Mohr, 1957–65.

Gaster, Theodore H., trans. and ed. *The Dead Sea Scriptures.* 2d ed. Garden City, N.Y.: Anchor Books, 1964.

Gaston, Lloyd. *No Stone on Another, Studies in the Significance of the Fall of Jerusalem in the Synoptic Gospels.* Supplements to *Novum Testamentum.* Leiden: E. J. Brill, 1970.

Genet, Jean. "Here and Now for Bobby Seale." *Ramparts* 8 (June 1970): 30–31.

Goguel, Maurice. "Jésus e le messianisme politique." *Revue historique* 142 (1929): 217–67.

Graham, Hugh Davis, and Gurr, Ted Robert, eds. *Violence in America: Historical and Comparative Perspectives.* New York: Bantam, 1969.

Grant, Robert. *A Historical Introduction to the New Testament.* New York: Harper & Row, 1963.

Gustafson, James M. *Christ and the Moral Life.* New York: Harper & Row, 1968.

———. "The Place of Scripture in Christian Ethics: A Methodological Study." *Interpretation* 24 (1970): 430–55.

Guzman, German. *Camilo Torres.* Trans. John D. Ring. New York: Sheed and Ward, 1969.

Haenchen, Ernst, "Die Komposition von Mk viii 27–ix 1 und Par." *Novum Testamentum* 6 (1963): 81–100.

————. *Der Weg Jesu.* Sammlung Töpelmann. 2. Reihe. Bd 6. Berlin: Töpelmann, 1966.

Hahn, Ferdinand. *Mission in the New Testament.* Studies in Biblical Theology 47. Trans. Frank Clarke. London: SCM, 1965.

Hatch, Edwin. *Essays in Biblical Greek.* Oxford: Clarendon, 1889.

Hengel, Martin, Review of *Jesus and the Zealots* by S. G. F. Brandon. *Journal of Semitic Studies* 14 (1963): 231–41.

————. *Die Zeloten.* Köln: S. J. Brill, 1961.

Hoskyns, Edwin C. *The Fourth Gospel.* Ed. Francis N. Davey. 2 vols. London: Faber and Faber, 1939.

Howard, George. "Romans 3:21–31 and the Inclusion of the Gentile World." *Harvard Theological Review* 63 (1970): 223–33.

Jack, J. W. *The Historic Christ.* London: James Clarke, 1933.

Jackson, F. J., and Lake, Kirsopp, eds. *The Beginnings of Christianity.* Pt. I: *The Acts of the Apostles.* 5 vols. New York: Macmillan, 1920–33.

Jeremias, Joachim. *The Parables of Jesus.* Trans. S. H. Hooke. New Testament Library. London: SCM, 1963.

Jones, LeRoi. *Home.* New York: Morrow, 1966.

Josephus, Flavius. *The Jewish War. Life. Against Apion. Jewish Antiquities.* Trans. and ed. H. St. John Thackeray, R. Marcus, A. Wikgren, and L. H. Feldman. 9 vols. Loeb Classical Library. London: Heinemann, 1926–65.

Kähler, Martin. *The So-Called Historical Jesus and the Historic Biblical Christ.* Trans., ed. and intro. Carl E. Braaten. Philadelphia: Fortress, 1964.

Käsemann, Ernst, "Principles for the Interpretation of Romans 13." *New Testament Questions for Today.* Trans. H. J. Montague and W. F. Bunge. London: SCM, 1969.

Kaiser, Otto, and Kümmel, W. G. *Exegetical Method.* Trans. and intro. E. V. N. Goetchius. New York: Seabury, 1967.

Keck, Leander E. "Mark 3:7–12 and Mark's Christology." *Journal of Biblical Literature* 84 (1965): 341–58.

Kittel, Gerhard, ed. *Theological Dictionary of the New Testament.* 6 vols. (to date). Trans. and ed. G. W. Bromiley et al. Grand Rapids, Mich.: W. B. Eerdmans, 1964–68.

Klausner, Joseph. *Jesus of Nazareth.* Trans. Herbert Danby. New York: Macmillan, 1929.

Klijn, A. F. J. *Edessa, die Stadt des Apostels Thomas. Das älteste*

164   BIBLIOGRAPHY OF WORKS CITED

Christentum in Syrien. Neukirchener Studienbücher. Ergänzungs-
bände zu den biblischen Studien. Bd. 4. Übersetzung v. Manfred
Hornschuh. Neukirchen-vluyn: Verlag des Erziehungsvereins, 1965.
Knigge, Heinz-Dieter. "The Meaning of Mark." *Interpretation* 22
(1968): 53–70.
Knox, John. *The Death of Christ*. New York: Abingdon, 1958.
Koester, Helmut. "GNŌMAI DIAPHOROI." *Harvard Theological Re-
view* 58 (1965): 279–318.
———. Review of *Das Geschichtsverständnis des Markusevangeliums*
by J. M. Robinson. In *Verkündigung und Forschung*. Theologische
Jahresbericht. München: Chr. Kaiser, 1959.
———. "One Jesus and Four Primitive Gospels." *Harvard Theological
Review* 61 (1968): 203–47.
Kümmel, W. G. *Introduction to the New Testament*. Trans. A. J.
Mattill, Jr. New York: Abingdon, 1966.
———. *Promise and Fulfillment*. Studies in Biblical Theology 23. Trans.
Dorothea M. Barton. London: SCM, 1957.

Lake, Kirsopp, and Cadbury, H. J. *The Beginnings of Christianity*.
Vol. 4. London: Macmillan, 1933.
Liddell, Henry G., and Scott, Robert. *A Greek-English Lexicon*. 9th ed.
2 vols. Rev. H. S. Jones and R. McKenzie. Oxford: Clarendon,
1925, 1940.
Lightfoot, R. H. *The Gospel Message of St. Mark*. Oxford: Clarendon,
1950.
———. *Locality and Doctrine in the Gospels*. London: Hodder &
Stoughton, 1938.
Linnemann, Eta. "Der (wiedergefundene) Markusschluss." *Zeitschrift
für Theologie und Kirche* 66 (1969): 255–87.
Little, David. "Is the War in Vietnam Just?" *Reflection* 64 (1966): 1–5.
———. "Six on Vietnam." *Worldview* 13 (1970): 6–11.
Lohmeyer, Ernst. *Das Evangelium des Markus*. 10th ed. Meyers kritisch-
exegetischer Kommentar über das Neue Testament. Göttingen:
Vandenhoeck & Ruprecht, 1937.
———. *Galiäa und Jerusalem*. Göttingen: Vandenhoeck & Ruprecht,
1936.
Loisy, A. *Le Quatrième Évangile*. Paris: Alfonse Picard et Fils, 1903.
Lorenz, Konrad. *On Aggression*. Trans. Majorie K. Wilson. New York:
Harcourt, Brace & World, 1966.
Luthuli, Albert. *Let My People Go*. New York: McGraw-Hill, 1962.

Luz, Ulrich. "Das Geheimnismotif und die markinische Christologie." *Zeitschrift für die neutestamentliche Wissenschaft* 56 (1965): 9–30.

Macgregor, G. H. C. *The Gospel of John.* Moffatt New Testament Commentary. London: Hodder & Stoughton, 1933.

Machiavelli, N. *The Prince and Other Discourses.* Ed. Max Lerner. New York: Modern Library, 1950.

Mandelkern, Solomon, ed. *Veteris Testamenti: Concordantiae Hebraicae atque Chaldaicae.* Lipsiae: Margolin, 1925.

Manson, T. W. *The Servant-Messiah.* Cambridge: University Press, 1953.

Marxsen, Willi. *Introduction to the New Testament.* Trans. G. Buswell. Philadelphia: Fortress, 1968.

————. *Mark the Evangelist.* Trans. James Boyce, Donald Juel, Wm. Poehlmann, with Roy A. Harrisville. New York: Abingdon, 1969.

————."Redaktionsgeschichtliche Erklärung der sogennanten Parabeltheorie des Markus," *Zeitschrift für Theologie und Kirche* 52 (1955): 255–71.

Mead, George H. *Mind, Self and Society.* Chicago: University of Chicago Press, 1934.

Merton, Thomas. *Faith and Violence.* Notre Dame, Ind.: University, 1968.

Michel, Otto. *Der Brief an die Römer.* 11th ed. Meyers kritisch-exegetischer Kommentar über das Neue Testament. Göttingen: Vandenhoeck & Ruprecht, 1957.

Mills, C. Wright. *The Causes of World War III.* New York: Simon & Schuster, 1958.

Montefiore, C. G. *The Synoptic Gospels.* 2d ed. 2 vols. London: Macmillan, 1927.

Morris, Colin. *Unyoung, Uncoloured, Unpoor.* London: Epworth, 1969.

Morse, Arthur D. *While Six Million Died: A Chronicle of American Apathy.* New York: Random House, 1968.

Nestle, D. E., and Aland, K., eds. *Novum Testamentum Graece.* 25th ed. Stuttgart: Württembergische Bibelanstalt, 1963.

Neusner, Jacob. *A Life of Rabban Yohanan ben Zakkai.* Studia Post Biblica Sextum. Leiden: E. J. Brill, 1962.

Niebuhr, H. Richard. *Christ and Culture.* New York: Harper & Row, 1951.

————. *The Responsible Self.* Intro. James M. Gustafson. New York: Harper & Row, 1963.

Niebuhr, Reinhold. *Christianity and Power Politics.* New York: Scribner's, 1940.

――――. *An Interpretation of Christian Ethics.* New York: Harper & Row, 1935.

――――. "Our Schizoid Vietnam Policy." *Christianity and Crisis* 26 (1967): 313–14.

――――. "The President on 'The Arrogance of Power.'" *Christianity and Crisis* 26 (1966): 125–26.

――――. "Vietnam: The Tide Begins to Turn." *Christianity and Crisis* 26 (1966): 221–22.

Nieburg, H. L. *Political Violence.* New York: St. Martin's, 1969.

Nineham, D. E. *The Gospel of St. Mark.* Pelican Gospel Commentaries. London: A. & C. Black, 1963.

Nygren, Anders. *Commentary on Romans.* Trans. Carl C. Rasmussen. Philadelphia: Muhlenberg, 1949.

Ogle, Arthur Bud. "Mister Little—The Answer is 'No!'" *Reflection* 64 (1967): 1–4.

Perrin, Norman. "The Wredestrasse Becomes the Hauptstrasse: Reflections on the Reprinting of the Dodd Festschrift." *Journal of Religion* 46 (1966): 296–300.

Potter, Ralph B. *War and Moral Discourse.* Richmond, Va.: John Knox, 1969.

Quispel, G. "Der Heiland und das Thomasevangelium." *Vigiliae Christianae* 16 (1962): 121–53.

――――. "The Latin Tatian or the Gospel of Thomas in Linburg." *Journal of Biblical Literature* 88 (1969): 321–30.

――――. "Some Remarks on the Gospel of Thomas." *New Testament Studies* 5 (1958–59): 276–90.

Ramsey, Paul. "Discretionary Armed Service." *Worldview* 10 (1967): 8–11.

――――. "From Princeton, With Love." *Reflection* 64 (1967): 5–6.

――――. "Is Vietnam a Just War?" *Dialog* 6 (1967): 19–29.

――――. *War and the Christian Conscience. How Shall Modern War Be Conducted Justly?* Durham, N. Car.: Duke, 1961.

Ringgren, Helmer. *The Faith of Qumran.* Trans. Emilie T. Sander. Philadelphia: Fortress, 1963.

Robertson, A. T. *A Grammar of the Greek New Testament in the Light of Historical Research.* 2d ed. New York: Hodder & Stoughton, 1915.

Robinson, James M. "The Coptic Gnostic Library Today." *New Testament Studies* 14 (1968): 356–401.

———. Intro. *The Quest of the Historical Jesus* by A. Schweitzer. Trans. Wm. Montgomery. New York: Macmillan, 1968.

———. *The Problem of History in Mark.* 2d ed. London: SCM, 1957.

———. "The Problem of History in Mark, Reconsidered." *Union Seminary Quarterly Review* 20 (1965): 131–47.

Rubinstein, Arie. "Observations on the Old Russian Version of Josephus' *Wars.*" Journal of Semitic Studies 2 (1957): 329–48.

Ryan, J. A., and Boland, F. J. *Catholic Principles of Politics.* New York: Macmillan, 1940.

Sanday, William, and Headlam, A. C. *The Epistle to the Romans.* International Critical Commentary. Edinburgh: T. & T. Clark, 1895.

Sandmel, Samuel *The First Christian Century in Judaism and Christianity.* New York: Oxford, 1969.

Schlatter, Adolf. *Der Evangelist Matthäus.* 4th ed. Stuttgart: Calwer, 1957.

———. *Die Geschichte Israels von Alexander dem Grossen bis Hadrian.* 3d ed. Stuttgart: Calwer, 1925.

Schlesinger, Arthur, Jr. *A Thousand Days.* Boston: Houghton Mifflin, 1965.

Schmidt, K. L. *Der Rahmen der Geschichte Jesu.* Darmstadt: Wissenschaftliche Buchgesellschaft, 1969 (reprinted from 1919 ed.).

Schmithals, W. *Paul and James. Studies in Biblical Theology* 46. Trans. Dorothea M. Barton. London: SCM, 1965.

Schnackenburg, Rudolf. *The Gospel According to St. John.* Vol. 1. Trans. Kevin Smith. Montreal: Palm, 1968.

Schniewind, Julius. *Das Evangelium nach Matthäus.* 11th ed. Das Neue Testament Deutsch. Göttingen: Vandenhoeck & Ruprecht, 1964.

Schoeps, H. J. *Jewish Christianity.* Trans. Douglas R. A. Hare. Philadelphia: Fortress, 1969.

———. Review of *The Fall of Jerusalem* by S. G. F. Brandon. *Journal of Ecclesiastical History* 3 (1952): 101–3.

———. *Theologie und Geschichte des Judenchristentums.* Tübingen: J. C. B. Mohr, 1949.

Schonfield, Hugh. *The Passover Plot.* New York: Bantam, 1967.

Schreiber, Johannes. "Die Christologie des Markusevangeliums." *Zeitschrift für Theologie und Kirche* 58 (1961): 154–83.

Schrenk, Gottlieb. "biazomai, biastēs," In *Theological Dictionary of the New Testament.* Ed. G. Kittel. Trans. & ed. G. W. Bromiley and others. Vol. I. Grand Rapids, Mich.: Wm. B. Eerdmans, 1964.

Schubert, Kurt. *The Dead Sea Community*. London: A. & C. Black, 1959.

Schürer, Emil. Review of *Die Zeugnisse von Christentum im slavischen "De bello judaico" des Josephus* by A. Berendts. *Theologische Literaturzeitung* 3 (1906): cols. 262–66.

Schweitzer, Albert. *The Mystery of the Kingdom of God*. Trans. & intro. Walter Lowrie. New York: Dodd & Mead, 1914.

———. *The Quest of the Historical Jesus*. Trans. Wm. Montgomery. Intro. James M. Robinson. New York: Macmillan, 1968.

Schweizer, Eduard. "Zur Frage der Messiasgeheimnis bei Markus." *Zeitschrift für die neutestamentliche Wissenschaft* 56 (1965): 1–8.

———. *The Good News According to Mark*. Trans. Donald H. Madrig. Richmond, Va.: John Knox, 1970.

———. "Mark's Contribution to the Quest of the Historical Jesus." *New Testament Studies* 10 (1963–64): 421–32.

Smith, Morton. "Zealots and Sicarii, Their Origins and Relation." *Harvard Theological Review* 64: (1971): 1–19.

Smylie, James H. "American Religious Bodies, Just War, and Vietnam." *Journal of Church and Society* 11 (1969): 383–408.

Sorenson, Theodore. *Kennedy*. New York: Harper & Row, 1965.

Stendahl, Krister. "Matthew." In *Peake's Commentary on the Bible*. 2d ed. Ed. M. Black and H. H. Rowley. New York: Nelson, 1962.

———. *The School of St. Matthew*. 2d ed. Philadelphia: Fortress, 1968.

Strecker, Georg. "The Passion and Resurrection Predictions in Mark's Gospel." *Interpretation* 22 (1968): 421–31.

———. "William Wrede. Zur hundertsten Wiederkehr seines Geburtstages." *Zeitschrift für Theologie und Kirche* 57 (1960): 67–91.

Streeter, B. H. *The Four Gospels*. London: Macmillan, 1924.

Stringfellow, William. "An Authority over Death." *Christianity and Crisis* 30 (1970): 181–83.

Szulc, Tad. and Meyer, Karl E. *The Cuban Invasion: The Chronicle of Disaster*. New York: Ballantine, 1962.

Talbert, C. H. *Luke and the Gnostics*. New York: Abingdon, 1966.

Taylor, Vincent. *Behind the Third Gospel*. Oxford: Clarendon, 1926.

Tertullian, Quintus S. F. *De Idololatria. The Ante-Nicene Fathers*. Ed. Alexander Roberts and James Donaldson. Vol. 3. Grand Rapids, Mich.: Wm. B. Eerdmans, 1968 (reprinted).

Throckmorton, B. H., et al., eds. *Gospel Parallels*. New York: Nelson, 1949.

Tillich, Paul. *The Theology of Culture*. New York: Oxford, 1959.

Tödt, H. E. *The Son of Man in the Synoptic Tradition.* Trans. Dorothea M. Barton. London: SCM, 1965.

Vielhauer, Philipp. "On the 'Paulinism' of Acts." In *Studies in Luke-Acts.* Ed. Leander E. Keck and J. Louis Martyn. Trans. William C. Robinson and V. P. Furnish. New York: Abingdon, 1966.

Violence in Southern Africa: A Christian Assessment. London: SCM, 1970.

West, Charles. *Ethics, Violence and Revolution.* New York: Council on Religion and International Affairs, 1969.

Westcott, B. F. *The Gospel Accordng to St. John.* 2 vols. London: John Murray, 1908.

Wheeler-Bennett, John W. *The Nemesis of Power.* 2d ed. New York: St. Martin's, 1967.

Wilckens, Ulrich. *Weisheit und Torheit.* Beiträge zur historischen Theologie 26. Tübingen: J. C. B. Mohr, 1959.

Wink, Walter. "Jesus and Revolution: Reflections on S. G. F. Brandon's *Jesus and the Zealots.*" *Union Seminary Quarterly Review* 25 (1969): 37-59.

Winter, Paul. *On the Trial of Jesus.* Berlin: Walter de Gryter, 1961.

Wrede, Wilhelm. *Das Messiasgeheimnis in den Evangelien.* Göttingen: Vandenhoeck & Ruprecht, 1901.

Yadin, Yigael. *Masada: Herod's Fortress and the Zealots' Last Stand.* New York: Random House, 1966.

Yoder, John H. *Karl Barth and the Problem of War.* Studies in Christian Ethics Series. New York: Abingdon, 1970.

Zeitlin, Solomon. *Josephus on Jesus.* Philadelphia: Dropsie College, 1931.

INDEX OF BIBLICAL REFERENCES

Old Testament

New Testament

GENERAL INDEX

(Numbers in parentheses indicate pages on which notes appear.)

175

Galilee, Galilean, 49, 53, 82
Gärtner, B., 36 n46(145)
Gaster, T. H., 87 n44(152)
Gaston, L., 62 n66(149)
Genet, J., 1 n1(141)
genre, of Gospel, 84
Germany, 11, 106, 109, 123
Gethsemane, 23, 29, 40
Gillette v. US, 121
Globe and Mail, Toronto, 116 n26(155)
gnostic, gnosticism, 71, 90-93, 95; gnostic redeemer myth, 65; Jewish gnosticism, 95
God of space/God of time, 96
Goguel, M., 30 n25(144)
Goldwater, B., 105 n6(154)
Good News Translation, 65
Good Samaritan, 101
Goodspeed, E. J., 65
Graham, Billy, 101
Graham, H. D., 3, 4, 10 n16(142)
Grant, F. C., 80, 81
Grant, R. M., 80 n26(151)
Greece, 18
Guatemala, 8
Gurr, T. R., 3 n8(141), 4, 10 n16(142)
Gustafson, J. M., *Christ and the Moral Life*, 113, 114 n17(154); *Interpretation*, 114 n19-20(154-55); *The Responsible Self*, 132, 133 n45-46(156)
Guzman, G., 127, 128 n38(155)

Habash, G., 42, 43n68(145)
Haenchen, E., *NT*, 80 n25(151); *Der Weg Jesu*, 38 n53(145), 51 n21(147)
Haggada of the Seder, 47, 49

Hahn, F., 64 n75(149)
Hahn, O., 107-8
Halosis, 25, 27, 29, 30; see also Josephus, Slavonic
Hamel, J., 56 n40(148)
Hamilton, C., 4 n9(141)
Hananiah, J. ben, 52
harba, 12 n19(142)
Headlam, A. C., 46 n6(146)
Hegelian, 35
hellenistic, hellenism, 37, 46, 81, 86, 90
Hengel, M., 57; *JSS*, 28 n18(143), 58 n52(148); *Die Zeloten*, 28 n17(143)
Hermas, Shepherd of, 36, 111
Herod the Great, 36
Hesiod, 17
hidah, 92-93
hilasterion, 46
Hiroshima, 123
historical criticism, 135
historical line of questioning, 63, 68
history, "bad," 116
history writing, 116
Hitler, A., 14 n22(142), 15, 104 n4(154), 106, 109, 124
HMS, 3
Ho Chi Minh, 15
Hobbes, Thomas, 139
Holy of Holies, 46
Hoskyns, E. C., 65 n76(149)
Howard, G., 46 n9(146), 47
Humanism, 100
Hungary, 19

Imitation of Christ, 130-36
Indians, American, 10
indicative/imperative, 91

180 GENERAL INDEX

individualistic, 101
insurrection, the, 24, 26
interim ethic, 131
internationalism, 109; *see also*
ecumenism; universal
Islam, 100
Israel, Israeli, 11, 42, 139

Jack, J. W., 27 n14(143), 28
Jackson, F. J. F., 56 n45(148),
57 n47(148)
Jackson State College, 2
Jahwist, 96
Jairus' daughter, 151
James, brother of Jesus, 35;
Epistle of, 132
Jamnia, 53
Jeremias, J., 81 n30-31(151), 92
n55(153)
Jesus of history, historical Jesus,
15, 16, 21-23, 25, 26, 29, 30, 38-
41, 50, 58-69, 80, 86, 91, 97, 99,
101, 135 (and Christ of faith),
136; messianic consciousness of,
40, 72, 85-88; the pacific Jesus,
15, 34, 38, 41, 64; violence of,
9, 12, 15, 16, 23, 29, 59, 68; *see
also* Christ; messiah; Son of
Man
Jewish Christianity, Jewish Chris-
tians, 23, 30-37, 39, 41, 45, 46,
58, 59, 61, 62, 79
Jews during World War II, 123-24
Johanan ben Zakkai, 52-53
John the Baptist, 3, 25, 27, 81
n28(151), 83
Johnson, Hewlett, 56
Jonas, H., 30 n26(144)
Jones, L., 9 n15(142), 10
Josephus, F., 23-25, 27, 28, 56,

60; *Antiquities*, 43 n71(146),
63 n74(149); *War*, 25, 31, 32,
43 n71(146), 44 n1(146), 45, 51
n20(147), 56 n45(148), 63
n74(149); Eisler and the Slavonic Josephus, 24, 25, 27, 28,
45, 60; Slavonic Josephus, 24,
25, 26 n8(143), 27, 28, 45, 60
Judas the Galilean, 50, 51, 56
just war, *see* war
justification by faith, 47

Kähler, M., 79 n19(150)
Kahn, H., 126
kalamos, 58
Käsemann, E., 54 n36(147)
Keck, L. E., 81 n29(151), 82
n34(152), 91, 92 n54(153)
Kent State University, 2
King James Version, 57, 65
King, Martin Luther, 128
kingdom of God, 9, 13, 47, 72
Klausner, J., 3 n5(141)
Klijn, A. F. J., 36 n48(145)
Knigge, H.-D., 81 n28(151), 91
knowledge, *gnōsis*, 90, 94
n59(153), 95 n60(153); *see also*
gnostic, gnosticism
Knox, J., *The Death of Christ*,
88 n46(152)
Koch, Rep. Edward, 119
Koester, H., *HTR*, 36 n47-
48(145), 84 n37(152); *Verk-
undigung*, 77 n14(150)
Korea, 18, 19
Ku Klux Klan, 68
Kümmel, W. G., *Introduction
to the New Testament*, 49
n14(146); *Promise and Fulfil-
ment*, 3 n6(141)

pacifism, 120; *see also* Christ,
the pacific; Jesus, the pacific
Palestine, Palestinian, 11, 39, 40,
42, 43, 49, 52, 53, 68, 70
Papias, 49
parable, parabolic, 92, 95; para-
ble as riddle, 92, 93
paradidonai, 82 n33(152)
passion narrative with extended
introduction, 71, 79, 89, 97
patriotic, 58; *see also* nationalism
Paul, Pauline, 34, 35, 46, 57, 89-
92, 101, 132
peace churches, 121
Pella, 30-33
Pentagon, Pentagonism, 125, 126;
Pentagon Papers, 6
Perrin, N., 80 n25(151)
Peter, Petrine, 34-36, 40, 49, 72,
80, 85, 86, 94, 95, 111
Pharisees pharisaism, pharisaical,
38-40, 82
Pilate, Pontius, 22, 24, 26
Ping Pong diplomacy, 124
Pompey, 50
Popular Front for the Liberation
of Palestine, 42, 43
Potter, R. B., 123 n35(155)
Poverty, 5, 104, 127
power, 16-20, 97, 107
Protestant, protestantism, 56,
129, 132
Proto-Luke, 48 n12(146)
Provenance of Mark, 48-50
Provenance of Matthew, 30-37
Psychology of adjustment, 101,
102
psychology, group, 104
psychotherapy, 103, n3(153)

Q source, 38-40, 44, 58, 88
qana, 58 n51(148)
Quirinius, P. S., 50 n19(147)
Quispel, G., *JBL*, 36 n4(145);
NTS, 12 n19(142); *VC*, 36
n48(145)
Qumran, 87, 94, 95; 1QH, 94
n59(153); 1QM, 87 n43(152);
1QS, 94; 1QSa, 87 n44(152)

racism, racist, 4, 68, 107; Special
Fund to Combat, 129
radical obedience, 133
Ramsey, P., 19 n29(142), 118,
119 n30(155)
rāz, 94, 95
Rechabites, 28, 29
redaction, redactional, 78, 80, 82,
84, 96; *see also* editorial
resurrection, 9, 12; physical resurrection, 85
revolution, revolutionary, 11, 13,
51, 53, 54, 67, 90, 102; just revolution, 118, 127-30; nonviolent
revolution, 54, 117
Rhodesia, 13, 128
Ringgren, H., 87 n44(152)
Robertson, A. T., 65 n77(149)
Robinson, James M., *NTS*, 95
n60(153); *The Problem of History in Mark*, 77 n13(150);
USQR, 77 n14(150)
Rome, 3, 23, 26, 32, 42, 44, 45,
50, 52, 53, 60, 80, 98
Rousseau, J. J., 137, 138
Ruiz, G., 8
Russia, Russian, *see* Soviet
Ryan, J. A., 129 n42(155)

Saddok, 43